On

Exchange

An Adjudicative Commentary

AF797836

Sources in Early Modern Economics, Ethics, and Law

General Editors

Jordan J. Ballor, Acton Institute
Stephen J. Grabill, Acton Institute

The disciplines of economics, ethics, and law cannot be detached from a historical background that was; it is increasingly recognized, religious in nature. Economists Adam Smith and Léon Walras drew on the work of sixteenth- and seventeenth-century Spanish theologians who strove to understand the process of exchange and trade in order to better articulate subjective value, a dynamic theory of money, the role of the merchant, and the concept of marginal utility. Likewise, political theorists John Neville Figgis and Otto von Gierke drew on the work of sixteenth- and seventeenth-century Dutch, Swiss, German, and Spanish jurists and ethicists who articulated concepts that laid the foundation for federalist political structures, constitutionalism, popular sovereignty, natural-law jurisprudence, and limited government in the Western legal tradition. After a long period in which economics, ethics, and law became detached from theology, many economists, legal scholars, political theorists, and theologians now see the benefit of studying early modern economic, ethical, and legal texts in their full cultural, often religious, context. This series, *Sources in Early Modern Economics, Ethics, and Law*, provides first-ever English translations and editions of some of the most formative but previously inaccessible texts that shaped the disciplines of economics, ethics, and law in the early modern era and beyond. These inexpensive translations of seminal texts will make substantive contributions to contemporary interdisciplinary discussion.

Editorial Board

Alejandro Chafuen, Atlas Economic Research Foundation, USA

Ricardo Crespo, Universidad Austral and CONICET, Argentina

Samuel Gregg, Acton Institute, USA

Richard A. Muller, Calvin Theological Seminary, USA

Herman Selderhuis, Theological University Apeldoorn, The Netherlands

John Witte, Jr., Emory Law School, USA

Zhibin Xie, Tongji University, China

On

Exchange

An Adjudicative Commentary

Martín de Azpilcueta

Translated by Jeannine Emery

Introduction by Rodrigo Muñoz

CLP Academic

Grand Rapids · Michigan

Refo500

On Exchange: An Adjudicative Commentary

© 2014 by Acton Institute

Translated by Jeannine Emery

Cover image: Salamanca Cathedral from the water, Salamanca, Spain
License: Public Domain
Photo credit: Coque
URL: http://commons.wikimedia.org/wiki/File:Catedral_Salamanca.JPG
Inset photo: Wikimedia Commons (http://commons.wikimedia.org/wiki/File:Mart%C3%ADn_de_Azpilcueta.jpg)

All rights reserved. No part of this publication may be reproduced, stored in a retrieval system, or transmitted in any form or by any means, including electronic, mechanical, photocopying, recording, or otherwise without the prior permission of the publisher.

ISBN: 978-1-942503-00-2

CHRISTIAN'S LIBRARY PRESS

An imprint of the Acton Institute for the Study of Religion & Liberty

98 E. Fulton
Grand Rapids, Michigan 49503
Phone: 616.454.3080
Fax: 616.454.9454
www.clpress.com

Interior composition by Judy Schafer
Cover design by Peter Ho
Editorial management by Andrew M. McGinnis

Printed in the United States of America

CONTENTS

On Exchange: An Adjudicative Commentary

Sources in Early Modern Economics, Ethics, and Law

Series Introduction

Jordan J. Ballor
Stephen J. Grabill

For the same underlying reasons that moral theology is held in disrepute by many Western intellectuals, modern economists tend to glibly dismiss or even simply ignore the economic ideas of the scholastics, whether those of the twelfth or the seventeenth century. For many intellectuals nowadays, moral theology has come to signify a passé form of religious thinking that embraces irrationality and dogmatism, and economic historians—along with notable astrophysicists, geneticists, paleontologists, political analysts, philosophers, and ethicists—have all espoused this line of thought. Among the latter, in particular, the identification of scholastic economics (or the "canonical concept of market behavior," as it is sometimes called) with Aristotelian metaphysics and ecclesiastical authority has made modern economic professionals reticent or, at the very least unreceptive, to acknowledging any sophisticated analytical contribution to monetary and value theory by the Schoolmen or the Doctors—their sixteenth- and seventeenth-century heirs.

The severing of economic ideas from their original historical and metaphysical contexts becomes especially pronounced in the contemporary debate over the prehistory of economics. Invariably, most mainstream economic historians locate the birth of modern economics in Adam Smith, the mercantilists, and the physiocrats. For historian of economics Mark Blaug, the prehistory of economics begins with the seventeenth-century mercantilists and not, as the revisionists insist, with either the ancient Greeks or the medieval scholastics. He coins the term *pre-Adamite economics* to methodologically define and restrict the era of prehistory to Smith's immediate and direct historical precursors: the seventeenth-century mercantilists, the physiocrats, and the British free-trade writers of the eighteenth century.

The broader question of whether the prehistory of economics should start in the thirteenth century or much earlier is, in Blaug's estimation, "an afterthought."[1] An afterthought, we might infer, which could presumably surface information that would challenge positivist assumptions about human behavior and social cohesion and one that will yield few, if any, new insights into quantitative methods and models. Where the scholastics analyzed economic and commercial transactions as either ethical or legal matters involving the application of natural law to civil contracts, "it was the mercantilists," contends Blaug, "who, long before Adam Smith, broke with the canonical conception of market behavior as a moral problem and fashioned the concept of 'economic man.'" These mercantilists

> believed in the direct power of self-interest and in matters of domestic economic policy came near to advocating laissez-faire. Adam Smith was not the first to have confidence in the workings of the 'invisible hand.' Nor is it necessary to appeal to scholastic influences to account for his grasp of the determination of prices by demand and supply.[2]

1. Mark Blaug, *Economic Theory in Retrospect*, 5th ed. (Cambridge: Cambridge University Press, 1997), 29.

2. Blaug, *Economic Theory in Retrospect*, 31.

Regardless of whether it is necessary to appeal to scholastic influences to explain how Smith, in particular, understood price and value to be determined, such a determination does not speak to the wider issue of whether such seminal figures in the history of economics as Bernardo Davanzati (1529–1606), Hugo Grotius (1583–1645), Samuel von Pufendorf (1632–1694), Gershom Carmichael (1672–1729), Francis Hutcheson (1694–1746), Jean-Jacques Burlamaqui (1694–1748), Adam Ferguson (1723–1816), Ferdinando Galiani (1728–1787), Auguste Walras (1801–1866), and Léon Walras (1834–1910) were influenced by scholastic treatments of price and value. Neither does this judgment determine, for that matter, whether Smith's entire system of thought remains intelligible if the role he assigns to teleology, final causes, divine design, and virtue is disregarded as merely ornamental.[3] In this wider respect, therefore, the modern quibble over scholastic influences in Smith is a red herring because, as Langholm attests, it sidesteps serious historical investigation into the continuities and discontinuities between scholastic and modern economic ideas.[4] Furthermore, it also has the convenient side effect of

3. See James E. Alvey, "The Secret, Natural Theological Foundation of Adam Smith's Work," *Journal of Markets & Morality* 7, no. 2 (Fall 2004): 335–61. See also Paul Oslington, ed., *Adam Smith as Theologian* (New York: Routledge, 2011).

4. "From an analytical and terminological point of view," writes Langholm, "there is much of scholastic teaching that can be seen to have survived into modern economics. This is not surprising, since (at least if this observation is limited to our Western civilization) it was in the high Middle Ages that the foundations were laid for the kind of systematic reasoning about social relationships that has run on continually to the present day. Sometimes, as in the case of the fairness of the market price, it was deemed pertinent above to point out a subtle shift in the moral basis that supported an apparently unaltered doctrine. Elsewhere, where doctrines have changed as radically as in the case of lending at interest, the scholastics can still be credited with posing the terms of an ongoing argument. Therefore, it would seem that much of the old vessel remained to receive new content. The question is how completely it was ever emptied of the

downplaying the importance of teleology and natural theology in the thought of Smith himself and other seventeenth-, eighteenth-, and nineteenth-century political economists.

By methodologically constricting the prehistory of economics to the mercantilists and the physiocrats, as positivist historiographers commend, economic history congeals around such characteristically "modern" concerns as the concept of "economic man," self-interest, and the emancipation of economics from the so-called canonical concept of market behavior. This arbitrary limitation of which ideas and which people carry weight in economic history only serves to bolster twentieth-century positivist assumptions, particularly those of value neutrality and *homo economicus*, the assumption that humans act as rational and self-interested agents who desire wealth, avoid unnecessary labor, and seek to order their decision making exclusively around those goals. In the end, the modern reduction of the prehistory of economics to the seventeenth-century mercantilists can be put in the form of an Occam's razor-like question: Why appeal to scholastic influences to illumine modern notions of money, value, and price when all the basic elements of classical economics are already embedded in mercantilism?

---

ferment prepared for it in the medieval schools. This subject requires a book rather than a few lines. In fact, it has been the subject of many books, some of them provoked or inspired by Max Weber's ideas about religion and capitalism. For simplicity, let us recall that scholastic economics rested on three intellectual traditions. The first support was the tradition of the Bible and the Church Fathers with its emphasis on individual duty. The second was the tradition of the recently rediscovered Roman law with its emphasis on individual rights. The two traditions were made to balance briefly and precariously in the Thomist synthesis by means of a third support in Aristotelian social philosophy." See Odd Langholm, "Scholastic Economics," in *Pre-Classical Economic Thought: From the Greeks to the Scottish Enlightenment*, ed. S. Todd Lowry (Boston/Dordrecht/Lancaster: Kluwer Academic Publishers, 1987), 132–33.

The most straightforward reply is that seminal ideas, which include revolutionary economic ideas, never develop in intellectual, historical, religious, philosophical, or geographical vacuums. "Enlightened," secular reaction to the medieval Church's temporal jurisdiction and to theology's intellectual hegemony as the queen of the sciences has created a modern milieu in which scholars are no longer even aware of the historical influence that fundamental Christian doctrines have exerted in Western culture and university life.[5] From very early times, Christian theologians assumed that the application of patterns of discursive reasoning (as in the scholastic method, which was a method instituted by medieval Christian theologians and adapted and applied for subsequent centuries) could yield an increasingly accurate understanding not only of God's word and moral will but also of the created order itself.

Thus the systematic application of reason to a variety of intellectual undertakings, including economic problems, was not the invention of the Enlightenment. Rather, the application of reason within a coherent intellectual framework is the legacy of Christian scholasticism—the method of the medieval and early modern schools. The application of this scholastic method led to increased understanding of the world and human affairs, and spurred efforts to formulate logical explanations of regular occurrences in nature. "All things possess order amongst themselves: this order is the form that makes the world resemble God," wrote Dante in the *Divine Comedy*.[6] It can be argued that the specific application of scholastic method to economic problems became the seedbed for innovative ideas that, after much dialectical refinement, came to shape the world of modern

5. See Chris L. Firestone and Nathan Jacobs, eds., *The Persistence of the Sacred in Modern Thought* (Notre Dame: University of Notre Dame Press, 2012).

6. Dante, *Paradise*, trans. Anthony Esolen (New York: Modern Library, 2004), 1:103–5, p. 9.

economics. The truth of this statement does not rest on modernity's own understanding of its birth, development, or future trajectory but rather on the demonstrable "internal interconnections and affinities among ideas, their dynamism or 'particular go' (Lovejoy's phrase), and the logical pressures they are capable of exerting on the minds of those that think them."[7]

Assent to this claim, however, will require the positivist historian to reconsider not only the relationship between metaphysical schemata and intellectual traditions, which, in turn, will require an acknowledgement of the indispensable role of theological doctrines in the history of ideas,[8] but it will also require an admission that the recent detachment of economics from morality is itself a novelty, an aberration from a long-standing tradition within political economy itself.[9] In Alvey's judgment,

---

7. Francis Oakley, *Natural Law, Laws of Nature, Natural Rights: Continuity and Discontinuity in the History of Ideas* (New York and London: Continuum, 2005), 9.

8. See Oakley, *Natural Law, Laws of Nature, Natural Rights*, 13–34. See also the various essays in Oakley's *Politics and Eternity: Studies in the History of Medieval and Early-Modern Political Thought* (Leiden: Brill, 1999); Oakley, *Omnipotence, Covenant, and Order: An Excursion in the History of Ideas from Abelard to Leibniz* (Ithaca: Cornell University Press, 1984); Oakley, *Kingship: The Politics of Enchantment* (Oxford: Blackwell Publishing, 2006); and William J. Courtenay, *Covenant and Causality in Medieval Thought: Studies in Philosophy, Theology, and Economic Practice* (London: Variorum Reprints, 1984).

9. Broadly, on the historical constriction and positivism of contemporary economic thinking, see John D. Mueller, *Redeeming Economics: Rediscovering the Missing Element* (Wilmington, DE: ISI Books, 2010). See also Jeffrey T. Young, *Economics as a Moral Science: The Political Economy of Adam Smith* (Cheltenham, UK: Edward Elgar, 1997); James Alvey, "A Short History of Economics as a Moral Science," *Journal of Markets & Morality* 2, no. 1 (Spring 1999): 53–73; Ricardo F. Crespo, "Is Economics a Moral Science?," *Journal of Markets & Morality* 1, no. 2 (Fall 1998): 201–11; Peter J. Boettke, "Is Economics a Moral Science? A Response to Ricardo F. Crespo," *Journal of Markets & Morality* 1, no. 2 (Fall 1998): 212–19; and Crespo, "Is

> There are two major reasons why economics has become detached from moral concerns. First, the natural sciences came to be seen as successful, and the attempt was made to emulate that success in economics by applying natural science methods, including mathematics, to economic phenomena. Second, the self-styled economic science came to adopt positivism, which ruled out moral issues from science itself.[10]

It is the latter recognition, perhaps more than any other, that squares the revisionists off against the positivists in the debate over the prehistory of economics.

When the positivistic bias begins to be put aside and we look anew at works from earlier periods, we find the early modern era to be a rich source of intellectual ferment on economic, ethical, and legal and political topics. In the sixteenth and early seventeenth centuries, a small but influential group of theologians and jurists centered in Spain attempted to synthesize the Roman legal texts with Aristotelian and Thomistic moral philosophy. The movement began with the revival of Thomistic philosophy in Paris, where, as Camacho recounts, "Pierre Crockaert underwent an intellectual conversion from nominalist philosophy to the philosophy of Thomas Aquinas."[11]

Shortly before 1225, the year of Aquinas' birth, Aristotle's works on metaphysics, physics, politics, and ethics became available in the West, and, within the span of a generation, Aristotelianism, which had been brought to Europe by Arabic scholars, would

Economics a Moral Science? A Response to Peter J. Boettke," *Journal of Markets & Morality* 1, no. 2 (Fall 1998): 220–25; Jeffrey T. Young, *Economics as a Moral Science: The Political Economy of Adam Smith* (Cheltenham, UK: Edward Elgar, 1997).

10. Alvey, "A Short History of Economics as a Moral Science," 53.

11. Francisco Gómez Camacho, "Later Scholastics: Spanish Economic Thought in the Sixteenth and Seventeenth Centuries," in *Ancient and Medieval Economic Ideas and Concepts of Social Justice*, ed. S. Todd Lowry and Barry Gordon (Leiden and New York: Brill, 1998), 503.

be a serious contender in medieval thought. Thomas sought a rapprochement between the Greek philosophical tradition that Aristotle represented and the Christian divine ideas tradition articulated by the likes of Augustine, pseudo-Dionysius, and Bonaventure. In 1512, Crockaert published his commentary on the last part of Thomas' *Summa theologicae* with the help of a student, Francisco de Vitoria (ca. 1483–1546).[12]

Approximately two hundred years before Thomas was born, the *Corpus iuris civilis* of Justinian had been rediscovered and had become the object of academic disputation. However, the traditions of Roman law and Aristotelian and Thomistic philosophy existed in relative isolation from one other, at least until the early sixteenth century in Spain. "In the sixteenth and early seventeenth centuries," states Camacho, "a synthesis was finally achieved by that group of theologians and jurists known to historians of law as the 'late scholastics' or the 'Spanish natural law school.'"[13] Schumpeter concurs with this judgment and adds, "It is within their systems of moral theology and law that economics gained definite if not separate existence, and it is they who come nearer than does any other group to having been the 'founders' of scientific economics."[14] The Salamancans in particular, writes Moss,

12. Camacho, "Later Scholastics: Spanish Economic Thought in the Sixteenth and Seventeenth Centuries," 503.

13. Camacho, "Later Scholastics: Spanish Economic Thought in the Sixteenth and Seventeenth Centuries," 503.

14. Joseph Schumpeter, *History of Economic Analysis*, ed. Elizabeth Booty Schumpeter (Oxford: Oxford University Press, 1954), 97: "And not only that it will appear, even, that the bases they laid for a serviceable and well-integrated body of analytic tools and propositions were sounder than was much subsequent work, in the sense that a considerable part of the economics of the later nineteenth century might have been developed from those bases more quickly and with less trouble than it actually cost to develop it, and that some of that subsequent work was therefore in the nature of a time- and labor-consuming detour."

> were as interested in a general theory of how exchange rates between different currencies are formed as in explaining why a bill of exchange is worth more in one region of Spain than in another region. Was the agio or exchange premium evidence of usury and therefore immoral behavior on the part of merchants and traders, or rather something 'natural' governed by the basic laws of supply and demand?[15]

The case of this so-called School of Salamanca is just one example of the rich intellectual traditions that have far too often been ignored or downplayed by contemporary scholarship. The coherent intellectual framework of Christian scholasticism reverberates not only in the field of economics but also in the related areas of ethics and law. Thus, political theorists John Neville Figgis and Otto von Gierke drew on the work of a variety of sixteenth- and seventeenth-century Dutch, Swiss, German, and Spanish jurists and ethicists who articulated concepts that laid the foundation for federalist political structures, constitutionalism, popular sovereignty, natural-law jurisprudence, and limited government in the Western legal tradition.[16] The diversity and variety of relevant sources from this period is underscored by the contribution of Protestant scholars, who produced significant scholastic works as well as more occasional treatises. Much of the early Protestant thought on economics, ethics, and law attaches to their homiletical and exegetical work in addition to the achievements in systems of moral theology and philosophy. The Dutch Reformed legal thinker Johannes Althusius (1563–1638) stands as a representative example in this regard, and his contributions

15. Laurence S. Moss, "Introduction," in *Economic Thought in Spain: Selected Essays of Marjorie Grice-Hutchinson*, ed. Laurence S. Moss and Christopher K. Ryan (Brookfield, VT: Edward Elgar, 1993), xv.

16. On Johannes Althusius in particular, see Otto von Gierke, *The Development of Political Theory*, trans. Bernard Freyd (New York: Howard Fertig, 1966), 70; and John Neville Figgis, *Studies of Political Thought: From Gerson to Grotius, 1414–1625* (Cambridge: Cambridge University Press, 1907), 175–85.

to the development of Western legal and political traditions are becoming increasingly appreciated.[17] After a long period in which economics, ethics, and law became detached from theology, many economists, legal scholars, political theorists, and theologians now see the benefit of studying early modern economic, ethical, and legal texts in their full cultural, often religious, context.

The Sources in Early Modern Economics, Ethics, and Law series is the latest installment in the excavation of the mines of early modern theological thought on these topics. The aim of this series is to offer economists, intellectual historians, moral theologians, and graduate students in the fields of economics, economic ethics, economic history, banking history, political economy, and moral theology a useful and accessible collection of some of the most important early modern texts in the fields of economics, ethics, and law. Now, for the first time, the unabridged texts of works such as Martín de Azpilcueta's *Commentary on the Resolution of Money* (1556), Luis de Molina's *Treatise on Money* (1597), and Juan de Mariana's *Treatise on the Alteration of Money* (1609), as well as selections from larger works such as Johannes Althusius' *Dicaeologicae* (1617) and Girolamo Zanchi's *Omnium operum theologicorum* (1619) will be available as stand-alone volumes in English translation and in modern editions with scholarly annotations. We hope that the publication of these primary texts in a series of paperbacks will help to facilitate exploration of the continuities and discontinuities, agreements and disagreements, innovations and ruptures among

17. See, for instance, John Witte Jr., "A Demonstrative Theory of Natural Law: The Original Contribution of Johannes Althusius," in *Public Theology for a Global Society: Essays in Honor of Max L. Stackhouse*, ed. Deirdre King Hainsworth and Scott R. Paeth (Grand Rapids: Eerdmans, 2010), 21–36; and Thomas O. Hueglin, *Early Modern Concepts for a Late Medieval World: Althusius on Community and Federalism* (Waterloo, ON: Wilfrid Laurier University Press, 1999).

theological communities during the latter half of the sixteenth and the early seventeenth century.

The translations and modern editions (in conjunction with the introductions by leading authorities) will show the sophistication with which Christian thinkers from a variety of confessional and theological perspectives examined issues such as the role and responsibilities of the civil magistrates, the existence and efficacy of natural law, usury, and the ethics of moneylending, as well as the new process of using bills of exchange (*cambium per litteras*) to replace the cumbersome and dangerous transportation of metallic coins between commercial fairs, which led not only to new scholastic insights on interest, credit, and international trade but also to a much more comprehensive analysis of monetary exchange and banking practices than had been undertaken before. The texts will also address the questions as particular as why the same currency was worth more in one region than another area's currency, and, moreover, why the rate of exchange fluctuated between one area and the next. These moral and economic concerns, along with many others, will be addressed in detail throughout the course of the series by some of the leading, and heretofore underappreciated, authorities from the early modern era.

ABBREVIATIONS

CE	C. G. Herbermann et al., ed. *The Catholic Encyclopedia*. 17 vols. New York: The Encyclopedia Press, 1840–1916.
Cod.	*Corpus Iuris Civilis*, Codex.
Dec. Grat.	*Decretum Magistri Gratiani*. Vol. 1 of *Corpus Iuris Canonici*, 2nd ed., edited by Emil Friedberg. Leipzig: Bernhard Tauchnitz, 1879.
Dec. Greg.	*Decretalium D. Gregorii Papae IX*. In *Corpus Iuris Canonici*, 2nd ed., edited by Emil Friedberg, vol. 2, 1–928. Leipzig: Bernhard Tauchnitz, 1879.
Dig.	*Corpus Iuris Civilis*, Digesta.
DMA	J. R. Strayer, ed. *Dictionary of the Middle Ages*. 13 vols. New York: Scribner, 1982–86.
Inst.	*Corpus Iuris Civilis*, Institutiones.
Liber Sextus	*Liber Sextus Decretalium D. Bonifacii Papae VIII*. In *Corpus Iuris Canonici*, 2nd ed., edited by Emil Friedberg, vol. 2, 929–1124. Leipzig: Bernhard Tauchnitz, 1879.
NCE	*New Catholic Encyclopedia*. New York: McGraw-Hill, 1967–89.
PL	J.-P. Migne, ed. *Patrologia cursus completus: Series latina*. 221 vols. Paris: J.-P. Migne, 1844–65.

INTRODUCTION*

Rodrigo Muñoz

Martín de Azpilcueta: Biographical and Academic Profile

Martín de Azpilcueta y Jaureguizar (1492–1586),[1] known as Doctor Navarrus, earned a bachelor in theology degree at Alcalá University. Later, he completed his training in Toulouse, the most renowned center for juridical studies in France, where he

* This is a revised version of the introduction first published in *Journal of Markets & Morality* 7, no. 1 (2004): 175–91, and subsequently in Stephen J. Grabill, ed., *Sourcebook in Late-Scholastic Monetary Theory* (Lanham, MD: Lexington, 2007), 3–15.

1. The classical biographies are M. Arigita y Lasa, *El Doctor Navarrus Don Martín de Azpilcueta y sus obras: Estudio histórico-crítico* (Pamplona: J. Ezquerro, 1895); H. De Olóriz, *Nueva biografía del Doctor Navarrus D. Martín de Azpilcueta y enumeración de sus obras* (Pamplona: N. Aramburu, 1916). E. Tejero gathers information of biographical writings on Azpilcueta: "Los escritos sobre el Doctor Navarrus," in *Estudios sobre el Doctor Navarrus: En el IV centenario de la muerte de Martín de Azpilcueta*, ed. Gobierno de Navarra (Pamplona: Universidad de Navarra, 1988), 22–34.

received the degree of doctor in canon law (1518) and gained his first teaching experiences.

As of 1524, he had served in several canon law chairs at the University of Salamanca, and, together with Francisco de Vitoria, he renovated the juridical and theological thought of the day.[2] Some years later, in 1538, he was invited by the kings of Portugal and Spain to transfer to Coimbra University for a brief period, which extended until 1556 when he returned to Spain to devote himself entirely to his writings.

In June 1561, Martín was appointed defense counsel in the criminal proceedings brought against the Toledo archbishop Bartolomé de Carranza, a case that took him to Rome in August 1567, where, on account of his work as defense counsel, he was appointed advisor in the Supreme Penitentiary Tribunal on the initiative of Pius V and Charles Borromeo. He died in Rome at the age of ninety-three.

Although he worked in numerous disciplines, his most important contribution was in the field of canon law and morality. Among his numerous written works the most important is the *Manual de confesores y penitentes* because of its significance and influence with a complex writing process that originated in the concrete circumstances surrounding its first publication in 1549, and developed in consecutive stages until it achieved its final form (Salamanca, 1556). It was an immense publishing success. In the second half of the sixteenth century and first quarter of the seventeenth, it ran to eighty-one editions, with

2. In a work that contains many autobiographical notes, Azpilcueta himself says: "Nobody denies that I brought from Tolosa, in France, to the University of Salamanca . . . the solid and useful science of Canon Law. The same as, a year later, Francisco de Vitoria, as wise as he is pious, introduced an elaborate theology, studied at the University of Paris." See "Apologetic Letter from Martín de Azpilcueta to don Gabriel de la Cueva, Duque de Alburquerque," in *Comentario Resolutorio de Cambios*, introducción y texto crítico de A. Ullastres, L. Pereña, and J. Pérez Prendes (Madrid: Consejo Superior de Investigaciones Científicas, 1965), 43–44.

ninety-two more in revisions, versions, and abridgments. First written in Portuguese, then in Spanish, and finally in Latin, it was translated several times into Italian and French.[3]

As its title suggests, the *Manual* is a work directed to the pastoral aspect of penance. It deals with issues considered necessary for the administration of the sacrament. However, Doctor Navarrus's most important work extends beyond the genre of the *Sumas de penitencia*—a genre that originated at the end of the thirteenth century, was based on the precedent of the *libri poenitentiales* of the late Middle Ages with few doctrinal developments, and was organized alphabetically according to terms, much like a dictionary. Because of its systematic structure and doctrinal vigor, Azpilcueta's *Manual de confesores y penitentes* is considered a milestone in the emergence of moral theology as an autonomous discipline at the beginning of the seventeenth century.[4]

On Exchange: An Adjudicative Commentary is one of four appendices to this *Manual* and as such belongs to Navarrus's group of moral writings. In them, the author recommends guiding criteria for pastors and penitents and indirectly offers acute observations and an analysis of the economic reality of his time, which has recently attracted the attention of economic historians.

3. An almost exhaustive catalogue of the editions appears in E. Dunoyer, *L'Enchiridion confessariorum del Navarrus: Dissertatio ad lauream in facultate S. Theologiae apud Pontificium Institutum "Angelicum" de Urbe* (Pamplona: Gurrea, 1957).

4. Cf. Rodrigo Muñoz, *Moral y economía en la obra de Martín de Azpilcueta* (Pamplona: Ediciones Universidad de Navarra, 1998), 111–22; J. Theiner, *Die Entwicklung der Moraltheologie zur eigenständigen Disziplin* (Regensburg: F. Pustet, 1970).

The Scholastics and the Historiography of Economic Thought

Historians of economic thought have become increasingly interested in the moral literature of the second scholastic period, which looks into the economic practices of sixteenth-century commercial capitalism. Although such interest relates to the whole of scholasticism, it especially considers the authors of the late scholastic or second scholastic period, which peaked during the Spanish *Siglo de Oro*[5] with the so-called School of Salamanca.[6]

During the sixteenth century, there was a theological renaissance driven by the changes that gave way to a new social and cultural life that put an end to the medieval model. Together with specifically theological matters—the need for renovation and the later Protestant reforms that were the immediate antecedents to the Council of Trent—other factors were the new idea of man and society; the demographic expansion in Europe; the surge of modern national states; and the discovery of the New World, with a massive affluence of precious metals and new markets in the Indies. Circumstances in both the New World and the Indies soon had an effect on Spanish prices. These phenomena, together with the development of banking activities and new forms of payment, gave way to an increasing capital flow and to

---

5. The *Siglo de Oro* was a period of great prosperity, happiness, and achievement in Spain during the sixteenth and seventeenth centuries.

6. See Odd Langholm, *Economics in the Medieval Schools: Wealth, Exchange, Value, Money, and Usury According to the Paris Theological Tradition, 1200–1350* (Leiden: Brill, 1992); Murray N. Rothbard, *Economic Thought before Adam Smith: An Austrian Perspective in the History of Economic Thought*, vol. 1 (Brookfield, VT: Edward Elgar, 1995); A. del Vigo Gutiérrez, *Cambistas mercaderes y banqueros en el Siglo de Oro español* (Madrid: BAC, 1997); F. Gómez Camacho, *Economía y filosofía moral: la formación del pensameinto económico europeo en la Escolástica Española* (Madrid: Síntesis, 1998).

the growth of credit and speculative activity, all of which became a formidable challenge for moral theology.

The new theological genres included the works of the penitential pastoral and *De iustitia et iure* treatises, along with more specific ones such as Azpilcueta's *On Exchange*. In them, we find observations on monopolies, just pricing, taxes, banking or credit practices, currency markets, and so forth. The publishing of new essays and Joseph Schumpeter's *History of Economic Analysis* (1954), devoted largely to the scholastic doctors, have led some historians to defend the scholastic literature as an important precedent for the specifically scientific analysis of the economy and have even led them to think of its authors as founders of modern economics.[7] In this context, Azpilcueta's work plays a singular role. Perhaps his most original contribution, and what has most attracted economists, is precisely the quality of his analysis regarding the value of money, which is reflected in *On Exchange*.

In the final centuries of the Middle Ages the development of monetary doctrines had been driven by the expansion of commerce: the evolution of currency and alternative means of payment, the commercial fairs of Castile, and the consecutive consolidation and improvement of banking and financial activities.[8] In Navarrus's case in particular, the price revolution in Castile precipitated his writing.

---

7. A study of the main views in the debate may be seen in Muñoz, *Moral y economía en la obra de Martín de Azpilcueta*, 22–69. For an English summary, see Muñoz, "Scholastic Morality and the Birth of Economics: The Thought of Martín de Azpilcueta," *Journal of Markets & Morality* 4, no. 1 (2001): 14–42.

8. For monetary aspects, banking activity, and commercial fairs, see H. Lapeyre, *Une famille de marchands, les Ruiz* (Paris: Colin, 1955), 241–71, 475–501; R. Carande, *Carlos V y sus banqueros: La vida económica en Castilla (1516–1556)* (Madrid: Sociedad de Estudios y Publicaciones, 1965), 223–53, 295–349; F. Ruiz Martín, "La banca en España hasta 1782," in *El Banco de España: Una historia económica*, ed. A. Moreno Redondo (Madrid: Banco

In fact, the supply of precious metals from America caused one of the first consequences for the Castilian economy of the sixteenth century: steady price increases. E. J. Hamilton has tried to quantify this flux and to examine its effects on prices, salaries, and economic welfare.[9] He concluded that the importation of metal was the cause of the tripling of prices between 1501 and 1600. Other authors have mitigated Hamilton's statements (correcting calculations and adding other factors with inflationary effects and complementary information), but the critics have not offered other alternatives to the quantitative theory he espoused. Although there is not a univocal correspondence between the arrival of massive amounts of precious metals and the price increases, it is impossible to deny a causal relationship between these two elements.[10] In the midst of his attempts to devise contemporary explanations of this phenomenon, Hamilton underestimated scholastic reflection:

> Few Spaniards had sufficient education to compose a mercantilist tract and the clergy had little inclination for economic speculation. The vast majority of outstanding Spanish mercantilists before 1700 were ecclesiastics, little acquainted with either the economic literature or life of financially advanced nations. Their profession afforded them scant opportunity to acquire the intricate economic knowledge requisite to fathom foreign exchange.[11]

---

de España, 1970), 1–196; and P. Spufford, *Money and Its Use in Medieval Europe* (Cambridge: Cambridge University Press, 1989).

9. Cf. E. J. Hamilton, "Spanish Mercantilism before 1700," in *Facts and Factors in Economic History: Articles by Former Students*, ed. E. F. Gay (Cambridge, MA: Harvard University Press, 1932), 214–39; E. F. Gay, *American Treasure and the Price Revolution in Spain, 1501–1650* (Cambridge, MA: Harvard University Press, 1934).

10. Cf. J. Nadal Oller, "La revolución de los precios españoles en el siglo XVI: Estado actual de la cuestión," *Hispania* 19 (1959): 503–29.

11. Hamilton, "Spanish Mercantilism Before 1700," 230.

However, other studies subsequent to Hamilton's have shown the merits of the School of Salamanca's (including Azpilcueta's) analysis of the phenomenon of Castilian inflation. Dempsey, Ullastres, and Larraz, and some years later Marjorie Grice-Hutchinson, have defended Navarrus's role as a precursor of scientific economic analysis and have encouraged a closer examination of his formulation of the quantitative theory of money.[12]

With some precedents in Aristotle and the medieval tradition, Jean Bodin (1568) was considered the first to demonstrate the principal cause of inflation. Larraz, however, has pointed out how little space Bodin assigned to this issue and has defended Salamanca's primacy, proving two things: first, that Bodin was preceded by the Spanish natural lawyers and moralists; and, second, that the Spanish school's explanation was broader than the French school's because the latter only linked monetary mass to price level, while the Spanish considered, too, a third interdependent factor, namely, foreign exchange.[13]

The issue here is not merely establishing precedence in the formulation of the quantitative theory of money. Grice-Hutchinson has said from a more general perspective that it was Schumpeter who realized that, contrary to what the majority of economic historians before him had thought, the origins of economic analysis lay in moral philosophy more than in mercantilism.

12. B. W. Dempsey, "The Historical Emergence of Quantity Theory," *The Quarterly Journal of Economics* 50, no. 1 (1935): 174–84; A. Ullastres, "Martín de Azpilcueta y su comentario resolutorio de cambios: Las ideas económicas de un moralista español del siglo XVI," *Anales de Economía* 3–4 (1941): 375–409; 5 (1942): 51–95; J. Larraz López, *La época del mercantilismo en Castilla, 1500–1700* (Madrid: Atlas, 1943); Marjorie Grice-Hutchinson, *The School of Salamanca: Readings in Spanish Monetary Theory, 1544–1605* (Oxford: Clarendon Press, 1952). The work by Ullastres, which was published in two parts in *Anales de Economía*, is reproduced as an introduction in *Comentario Resolutorio de Cambios*, ed. Ullastres et al., 42–117.

13. Larraz, *La época del mercantilismo en Castilla* (Madrid: Aguilar, 1963), 86.

Regarding the School of Salamanca, Grice-Hutchinson notes its consistent originality in a triple contribution to monetary theory: its formulation, in the first place, of a psychological theory of value that may be applied both to goods as well as to money; in the second place, of a quantitative theory; and, finally, its formulation of a theory of foreign exchanges that is similar to the modern theory of the parity of buying power, a theory that we do not usually associate with the sixteenth century.[14]

Azpilcueta's *On Exchange*

We have already alluded to the social historical context of Azpilcueta's commentary by referencing the economic evolution of the sixteenth century. From an intellectual historical point of view, therefore, it is important to refer now to the problem of usury.

Doctrinal Context

The theory of usury is in many respects *sui generis* and of great significance for the scholastics' commercial ethics. The reason is that doctrinal developments—perhaps here more than in any other aspect of economic ethics—have a multisecular tradition: the biblical writings and Roman law texts were developed for the first time in the writings of the church fathers and shaped into the canonical legislation on usury, which extends for more than a thousand years. Often these sources are judged too hastily by moderns, and the medieval approach to the problem of usury is ruled out without paying very much attention to the economic reality of each period and to the arguments for why usury practices were considered unjust. As it is not possible to go into them in detail here, only a summary of their conceptual framework will be provided.[15]

14. Grice-Hutchinson, *The School of Salamanca*, 47ff.

15. I have written on the evolution of usury in the scholastics with some degree of thoroughness, focusing especially on Azpilcueta, in Muñoz, *Moral*

Usury is applied to the loan of things whose use is their consumption (*mutuum*), such as wheat, wine, money, and so forth. Any retribution was usurious if it was demanded for the use of a consumable good. The reason was that in such cases, because the use of the thing was inseparable from its consumption, the contract transferred the property, and the one who received it agreed to not give back the same thing—which was impossible—but an equivalent quantity and kind of what had been received. For this reason, demanding anything more than the loaned capital (*ultra sortem*) was considered usury. Some of the arguments used were that it was illicit to sell time; that money, unlike other things, did not deteriorate with use; and that there was an absence of risk for the lender, who turned the interest into a profit that did not compensate for the work or risk and was therefore unjustified. Renting a house or a field was different because they were not consumed by use and had to be restituted themselves together with their fruits, that is, they allowed for the payment of a rent. The profit gained from the use of consumable goods was a fruit not of the goods but of the work applied to them; a retribution for what was deemed "mere lapse of time" (*inter esse*) was not allowed. Saint Thomas Aquinas's example is instructive. He opposed giving money as a loan with giving

y economía en la obra de Martín de Azpilcueta, 203–337. For a synthesis of the biblical perspectives, see A. Bernard, "Usure. I. La formation de la doctrine ecclésiastique sur l'usure," in *Dictionnaire de Théologie Catholique*, ed. A. Vacant and E. Mangenot, 15 vols. (Paris: Letouzey et Ané, 1903–1950): 15:2316–17; and H. Lesêtre, "Prêt," in *Dictionnaire de la Bible*, ed. F. Vigouroux, 5 vols. (Paris: Letouzey et Ané, 1895–1912), 5:617–18. For a general perspective, see G. Le Bras, "Usure. II. La doctrine ecclésiastique de l'usure a l'époque classique (XIIe–XVe siécle)," in *Dictionnaire de Théologie Catholique*, 15:2336–72; the study by T. P. McLaughlin is magnificent: "The Teaching of the Canonists on Usury (XII, XIII, and XIV Centuries)," *Mediaeval Studies* 1 (1939): 81–147; 2 (1940): 1–22. Even if guided by a debatable presupposition, J. T. Noonan's work is a classic: *The Scholastic Analysis of Usury* (Cambridge, MA: Harvard University Press, 1957).

money to a merchant or artisan in order to constitute a society, or a commercial undertaking. In the case of a loan, there is a transference of ownership and risk for the loss of the thing, and, because of this, the lender should not ask for more. But the one who gives money to a merchant retains the property and risk, and may thus ask, as a fruit of the thing that belongs to him, for a part of the profit gained.[16]

In addition to this consideration, which was the essence of the scholastic doctrine on usury, there was a doctrine on *extrinsic titles*, that is, cases where payment was justified for reasons extrinsic to the *mutuum* contract. It was generally licit to pay a sum not as interest but for damage or loss to the lender (*damnum emergens*), as for example, a delay in fulfilling the contract. *Lucrum cessans* posed a more complex problem, and there were different opinions. In some authors, it is difficult to establish a clear distinction between the limits of a damage and the end of a profit or benefice. The development of this argument in the sixteenth century is interesting, in that it finally justified the payment of an interest only when the money is lent by a merchant, that is, by the one who gives money a productive use and undergoes an economic loss when lending. This is, for example, Azpilcueta's case: "More is owed to the merchant for the money he deals with than to another who does not deal with anything. The consequence of which is that money pays better in the hands of merchants and money changers who invest it 'actively' than in other hands in which it may end up being hoarded."[17]

Finally, among the extrinsic titles is risk (*periculum sortis*), considered not as the possibility of the borrower's insolvency so much as the risk of the possessions' loss. In many cases, the risk was related to the danger of a long voyage: pirates, theft,

16. Cf. *Summa theologicae*, II-II, q. 78, art. 2 ad 5.

17. Martín de Azpilcueta, *Comentario Resolutorio de Usuras* (Salamanca: Andrea de Portonarijs, 1556), p. 24–25, sec. 52.

shipwreck, and so forth. In any case, *periculum sortis* was unanimously rejected as a title to compensation.

Following Aristotle, the early scholastics had already reflected on money, but the morality of exchange operations became important with Saint Antonino de Florencia's work and was officially approved in the sixteenth century with the publishing of Cajetan's (1499) *De cambiis* (*On Exchange*). Later, the subject matter of treatments *de cambiis* became independent from the study of usury. Azpilcueta himself wrote a treatise about each of those issues, and published them as appendices to the *Manual*: the *Comentario Resolutorio de Usuras* and the *Comentario Resolutorio de Cambios* (Salamanca, 1556). The differences between the subjects have more to do with juridical criteria than with doctrinal criteria, since money exchange operations were considered insofar as they had a financing element and, thus by extension, were given the same moral treatment as usury.

As strange as the handling of this issue seems today, this is the formal structure behind the scholastic reflection on compensation for credit and other types of monetary exchange that are similar to it. We should remember the distance between the economic reality of those days—deficiencies in the monetary system, the lack of a productive destiny for capital, credit, and so forth—and today's economic realities.

The Economic Ideas of *On Exchange*[18]

The Concept of Exchange

The word *exchange* had two meanings for Navarrus. A general one, which the Romans called *permuta*, referred to the exchange

18. Parenthetical references are to the sections in Azpilcueta's commentary. A thorough analysis of the commentary may be found in Ullastres, "Martín de Azpilcueta y su comentario resolutorio de cambios" and in Muñoz, *Moral y economía en la obra de Martín de Azpilcueta*, 281–337. See also Bernard Gazier and Michèle Gazier, *Or et monnaie chez Martin de Azpilcueta* (Paris: Économica, 1978).

of one thing for another, including of money for money. In a restricted sense, the word applied to other contracts or the exchange of money for money that did not fit into the Roman law classification: some types of acquisition, rentals, and so forth. Thus, *exchange* meant "every kind of contract of money for money that is not gratuitous," be it acquisition, deposit, or any other (sec. 10).

The Different Uses of Money

Azpilcueta had no doubt about the need for money, and described the following eight uses (cf. sec. 11–12):

1. as a means of payment;
2. as a measure of the value of things;
3. as an employment in exchanges between coins of different metal, different value, or different places;
4. to display one's riches to others;
5. as an ornamental element in dress;
6. "to cheer with its presence";
7. "to cure some illnesses with its broth" (the broth of gold was thought to have therapeutic properties); and
8. as pawn for a debt.

Obviously, some of these uses did not have an economic content. Regarding its use in exchanges the author confronted Aristotle's negative opinion on the *crematistic* (the lucrative commerce with no limits, which is different from the exchanges made to satisfy domestic needs), which was, according to the philosopher, unnatural. The profit-based economy was for Aristotle a consequence of the invention of money. He illustrated it with an example: It was possible to give a double use to shoes: a natural one, as footwear, and an improper one as an object of exchange. Navarrus softened Aristotle's harsh opinion: As well as using shoes to trade with, using money in exchanges is not unnatural, even if it is a secondary use compared to the principal one. With this observation, the author put money on the same level as any other merchandise, and, consequently, established that the morality of exchanges did not depend on money as their object but on an equitable exchange (cf. sec. 13).

Types of Exchange

Taking into account the earlier classifications by Silvestre and Cajetan, Azpilcueta offered seven types of exchange, some of which were in these precedents.

Exchanging as a profession. More than simply an examination of a type of exchange, the author analyzed the licitness of the exchanger's occupation and his remuneration. He tended to accept it for the following reasons: (1) There is no usury if the payment rewards the work of the exchanger instead of the loan; (2) such profession is a service to the republic (common good), and the employees may receive a salary; and (3) if the money exchanger carries out a public function, it is just that he receive a retribution for it, and he may also receive payment by practicing the profession in private, although in this case there is a possibility of fraud.

Exchanging for small coinage. In regard to the exchange of large denomination coins for small denomination ones, or the opposite, the author considered it licit to charge something for the service, even if such activity might be prohibited to private exchangers for reasons of monetary policy.

Exchanging for bills of exchange. The increase of commerce together with the coin scarcity forced the creation of alternative means of payment and the use of paper. The commercial fairs of Castile played an important role in this process.[19] Azpilcueta referred to it as the "virtual transference of money" to another place by means of a bill of exchange (sec. 21). The author thought

19. Cf. Carande, *Carlos V y sus banqueros*, 338; B. Aguilera Barchet, *Historia de la letra de cambio en España, seis siglos de práctica trayecticia* (Madrid: Tecnos, 1988).

that this form of exchange could be licitly rewarded under the condition that the nominal price was equivalent to the sum rendered, since such payment compensated for the service rendered (the physical transportation of the money or the work involved to keep the money in a distant place) and not for the credit, in which case it would be a usurious practice (cf. sec. 23). The exchanges made for reasons of place (*ratione loci*) were admitted without exception. This was not the case with those made for reasons of time lapse (*ratione temporis*), which were considered usurious.

Exchanging by true transference. This expression referred to the physical transference of money, as opposed to its virtual transfer. The author referred to the acquisition of money in a certain place where it could be devalued for a certain reason, to take it where it would be exchanged for a higher price in order to obtain a profit in the two successive exchanges. This may be a primary form of what we know today as currency swapping. He believed that this type of exchange was licit as long as it was carried out for a just price and more or less money was not given for advancing or postponing the payment.

Exchanging for interest. The previously mentioned doctrine about extrinsic titles may apply here. The exchanger who by lending was harmed because of profit, loss, or damage could ask for compensation for the benefits that he renounced or for the damages suffered. The author added that merchants may charge more if the debt is due to the second fairs than if it is due to the first ones because the *lucrum cessans* is greater: "the exchanger who stops exchanging with his money for two fairs is prevented from earning more than if he stopped for one fair" (sec. 34). However, he went on to condemn the person who removed his money from the deal and transferred it from fair to fair for an interest that was equivalent to the amount he was used to gaining through commerce (sec. 35). The reason for condemning this practice was the previous abandonment of commerce, which eliminated the possibility of *lucrum cessans*.

Azpilcueta considered time lapse relevant as long as it affected the amount of the damage or profit/loss and, with it, the compensation owed to the lender. However, setting aside the issues pertaining to interest, the term for the credit could not be taken into consideration to establish a retribution for the capital, as this was a reprehensible moral activity.

Exchanging for safekeeping. This form of exchange consisted of the actual visible bank deposit, whereby the bank committed to making payments on behalf of the depositor. He believed it was a useful enterprise for the republic and one in which the exchanger could licitly be paid a salary because it is his occupation "to receive the money from the merchants; to deposit it; to have it ready; and also to write, keep the books, [and] give an account of the money to everyone" (sec. 36). The author cleverly condemned those who deposited with the exchanger and who "do not want to pay anything, saying that what the exchangers earn with their money and receive from those who pay in cash is enough of a salary. Then if the exchangers ask for something, they leave them and go deal with someone else, and so, in order to avoid this, the exchangers decide not to take a salary owed to them but take it from someone who does not owe it to them" (sec. 40).

Exchanging by buying, bartering, or innominate contract. This is described as if someone gave one hundred in Medina to receive one hundred ten in Flanders, or the other way around. Then, with a great deal of realism, Azpilcueta set aside the juridical-formal structure of contracts, stating that there were actually two things that could make an exchange unjust: "the inequality of what is given and what is to be received," and "taking more or less for advancing or postponing [the payment], or for giving a long or short term to pay it back" (sec. 41). Once rid of the formal juridical requirements (sec. 42–43), he tackled the main issue: "the difficulty is in declaring how a profit can be made by commuting money by giving the just value for it" (sec. 43).

The Value of Money: The Quantitative Element

Navarrus thought it was possible to establish the value of money by deciding when and how a currency, which was apparently equal to another, was worth more or less for a certain reason. He described eight factors that affected the value of money. It is worth noting that the author had an unstructured idea of money, tied to the monetary unit, whether in its nominal aspect or in the materiality of the metal, even if he went beyond the rigid notion of giving an immutable value to it. However, when evaluating his position, one should take into account the deficiencies of the monetary system in sixteenth-century Europe.

The eight factors that affected the value of money were:

1. the nonexistence of coins of the same metal;
2. metals of a different value;
3. the different shape and weight;
4. the diversity of the land in which they circulated;
5. decisions made by the authority relative to the context where the coin circulated or changes in the relationship between the legal value and the intrinsic value;
6. the diversity of time;
7. the lack and need of money; and
8. the presence or absence of different coins.

The first five factors of price variation address money's fluctuation between its purely metallic dimension and the nominal one. As for the time factor, the author admitted it was a purely accidental consideration, but one that had a relationship with other factors that affected money's value.

The quantitative aspect is more interesting. Azpilcueta noted that money changed its value in relationship with its quantity. If goods got costlier because of the great need for them and their scarcity, that is, because of supply and demand, money was not an exception to this rule. Navarrus's words are sufficiently explicit:

> All other things being equal, in those countries where there is a great lack of money, less money is given for marketable goods, and even for the hands and work of men, than where there is an abundance of it. This we can see from experience in France where there is less money than in Spain. Bread, wine, wool, hands, and work cost less. Even in Spain, when there was less money, much less was given for saleable goods, and the hands and work of men, than later when the discoveries of the Indies covered it in silver and gold. The cause for this is that money is worth more where and when there is a lack of it than where and when there is an abundance. That which some say, that the lack of money reduces the price of everything, is born of the fact that its more than sufficient increase makes everything appear much lower, just as a small man next to a very tall man appears smaller than if he were next to his equal. (sec. 51)

Azpilcueta transcended a notion of money based on the nominal and metallic aspects and established its value based on its relationship with goods. In other words, money derived its value from its buying power. Also, given a certain moment in time and without the influence of other factors, there was a proportional quantitative relationship between the total amount of money available and the volume of merchandise—including the "work of men"—that could be bought with that amount of money. The author's ideas may be summed up in three conclusions.

First, the abundance or scarcity of money affected the relationships that diverse sectors of the monetary system had among them, as well as the system itself considered in its totality—that is, the goods that could be acquired with these monetary units or with units of another system.

Second, the value of money could rise or fall, not only because it was metal but also because it was a price for other things (sec. 57). Money was considered something fixed when taken as a unit for counting, but its value was variable when considering the utility it brought to its possessor (sec. 58).

Third, Azpilcueta's clarity and his notion of money related to its buying power set him apart from the medieval theory that considered money as an invariable mass. After observing the phenomenon of Castilian inflation, Navarrus could no longer remain in that position. His observations were published twelve years before Jean Bodin's.

The Critical Text

The text, whose English translation follows, appeared as an appendix to *Manual de confesores y penitentes*[20] and was dedicated to the prince Don Carlos, son of Philip II.[21] The treatise—which follows one on usury—extends from page 48 to page 104 in the separately paginated appendix. The sections are numbered, and each chapter is preceded by a summary of subjects. This text presents a difficult orthography, with marginal notes in Latin and abundant abbreviations, and it corresponds to the 1557 edition in the Madrid National Library (R/18063) that is signed by Miguel de Azpilcueta, which suggests that the exemplar may have belonged to the author.

The maturity of Azpilcueta's ideas should be situated around 1530, when he was professor at Salamanca and engaged in commentary on the *Decreto* and the *Decretales* regarding usuries and exchanges. Indeed, *On Exchange: An Adjudicative Commentary* appeared, according to its title and continuing with the genre developed in the field of canon law, as a commentary on the first part of the well-known decretal *Naviganti*. However, it was actually a treatise on exchanges that far exceeded its function as a gloss on the decretal. After dealing successfully in its first pages with the problems raised in the decretal on the contract

20. Valladolid: Francisco Fernandez de Cordoua, 1570. The appendix has a publication date of 1569.

21. Cf. L. Pereña, "El comentario de cambios," in *Comentario Resolutorio de Cambios*, ed. Ullastres et al., 15–27.

of maritime insurance, the author offered a detailed analysis of the main points regarding the matter of *cambiis*.

The commentary was disseminated quickly. The last edition in Spanish, the tenth, was published in Valladolid in 1569. However, the work had already been translated into Portuguese (1560), Italian (1568), and Latin (by an unknown translator) (1569). In 1601 it was translated into French. In the 1573 Latin edition of the *Manual*, Azpilcueta disavowed the 1569 Latin translation because it contained "many things contrary to my thoughts."[22] He did not, however, include a translation of the commentary in the 1573 Latin edition, but rather provided a synthesis with some references to the Spanish edition in chapter 17, which he authorized as an interpretation of the 1556 edition. The Spanish text was not edited again, although the Latin edition was reproduced many times in the editorial centers of Europe. The responses of the author to an inquiry on the subject of exchanges, published posthumously in another volume in 1590,[23] are also of value, as they examine the application of these principles to tangible situations.

22. *Enchiridion siue manuale confessariorum et poenitentium* (Rome, 1573), epistle to the reader.

23. *Consiliorum siue responsorum Martini ab Azpilcueta Doctoris Navarri*, vol. 2 of *Consiliorum et responsorum libri quinque* (Rome, 1590), 435–38.

On

Exchange

An Adjudicative Commentary

THE TEXT OF *NAVIGANTI*[*]

In order to understand what we intend to say about exchanges in our time, we state the words of Gregory IX,[1] in the beginning of the last chapter of *de usuris*, which are as follows:

> The one who lends a certain quantity of money to someone sailing or going to a fair, because he took upon himself the danger, hoping to receive something beyond the capital, is to be thought a usurer.[2]

Notes

* This is a revised version of the translation first published in *Journal of Markets & Morality* 7, no. 1 (2004): 193–312, and subsequently in Stephen J. Grabill, ed., *Sourcebook in Late-Scholastic Monetary Theory* (Lanham, MD: Lexington, 2007), 17–107. The source for this translation is the critical edition of the early modern Spanish text, *Comentario Resolutorio de Cambios*, ed. Alberto Ullastres, José M. Pérez Prendes, and Luciano Pereña (Madrid: Consejo Superior de Investigaciones Cientificas, 1965), 3–105. Where the author has included text of a language other than Spanish (such as Latin or Italian), it has been the editors' practice to translate the text and place the original in a note. Except where indicated by "Ed. note," all notes are the author's, although the editors have silently added the names of authors and the full titles of some works to the author's notes, and have also regularly inserted modern references in brackets in order to clarify the original citations.

1. Ed. note: Gregory IX (1170–1241) was elected to the papacy in 1227. In addition to a strained relationship with Emperor Frederick II, Gregory's pontificate was marked by a continuous battle against heresy as indicated by the constitutions inserted into the *Corpus Iuris Canonici*, among which was included the ruling *Naviganti de usuris*. This famous ruling condemned all known forms of usury and became the starting point for subsequent learned discussion of the intricacies pertaining to usury doctrine throughout the medieval and early modern eras (*NCE*, s.v. "Gregory IX, Pope").

2. *Naviganti, vel eunti ad nundinas certam mutuans pecuniae quantitatem, eo quod suscepit in se periculum, recepturus aliquid ultra sortem, usurarius est censendus.* [*Dec. Greg.*, 5.19.19]

1

TEXT INTERPRETATION

Summary

If the person who takes upon himself the peril lends money to someone about to sail or transfers the money somewhere else is a usurer, and when he is such ... **1, 2**

And what will happen if he lends something that is not money ... **6**

This chapter has two interpretations, and which is the best one ... **1, 2**

The example does not restrict the rule ... **2**

If there is an affirmation about something, no denial is made of similar or contrary issues ... **2**

Gregory IX proves to be methodical, beneficial, and concise ... **2**

He often embarks upon uncertain issues ... **3**

This means it is the truth and should be considered ... **3**

What nautical usury is ... **3**

1. The first thing we say regarding Gregory IX's principle is that it has two interpretations. One belongs to the ancient doctors,[2] according to whom the words "because he took upon himself the danger"[3] should be joined to the participle "hoping to receive."[4] Thus, the wording should be arranged as follows: "The one who lends a certain quantity of money to someone sailing or going to a fair, hoping to receive something beyond the capital, because he took upon himself the danger, is to be thought a usurer."[5] This means what Panormitanus's[6] summary says, that is, that the person who receives more than what he lent is a usurer even if he assumes the risk.

The other interpretation belongs to some newer authors, which we, too, followed when we read them at this most distinguished University of Salamanca in the year 1530, according to whom the words "because he took upon himself the danger"[7] should go next to the participle "the one who lends."[8] The result of which is: "The one who lends a certain quantity of money, because he took upon himself the danger, to someone sailing or going to a fair, hoping to receive something beyond the capital, is to be thought a usurer."[9] This means that the person who lends money to whomever is about to head to dangerous places, under the condition that he insures it with the lender and gives him something more than the amount lent for the insurance, is a usurer.

Such is the way John Major[10] understands it, saying the gloss here is inaccurate. Such is the way Silvestre[11] also understands it, saying the Supplement did not analyze this text.

Such is the way it seems that Cajetan,[12] Medina,[13] and Soto[14] understand it.

This way of considering things makes it seem from the ancient doctors' interpretation that whoever insures a piece of merchandise that is to go through dangerous places is a usurer if he takes something for it, a practice that goes against all Christian custom, against a law that allows setting a price on insurance,[15] and against the general opinion.[16]

2. In the second place, we state that even if in the past we held this second interpretation because of this argument, now, however, that God allows us to judge the texts more maturely, we think the first interpretation that the gloss received given by everyone to it, is better, according to which the result is somewhat more judicious than that of the others,[17] and is as follows: The person who lends money to take it elsewhere (even if he takes the danger upon himself), should be judged a usurer if he takes for himself more than what he lent.

This is supposed to be a general summary, because even if the text only refers to the person who lends to the merchant or to the one who goes to the fairs the summary refers to him and to whomever lends to anyone who will take it elsewhere. The text does not refer to the person who lends to the merchant or to the one who goes to the fairs to indicate that this does not occur with other lenders but as a mere example or to say that it occurs with them for more important reasons.[18] If someone who lends to a person who is to undergo a sea voyage (where there are generally more dangers) is not excused of usury even if he assumes the dangers, there is less excusing the person who assumes the dangers and lends to someone who will undergo fewer perils.

If the lender of the person who goes to the fairs, often a merchant who borrows in order to make a bigger profit when he goes to the fairs by buying merchandise, is not excused, then he is even less excused if he lends to someone who is in more unfortunate circumstances.

Third, this summary and this interpretation confirm the following:

- This is the way it has been interpreted by all those who have explained it here.
- The structured text of this principle is very clear on this and cannot say what others would like to interpret without constructing it in a way that is obviously forcing the argument, as would probably happen if a person reconstructs it according to the two interpretations in an impartial way.
- This text is structured by Gregory IX, and, as such, is methodical, beneficial, concise, and well analyzed, without inaccuracies or strange constructions, and out of one hundred learned men in Latin composition who read this text—without taking into consideration whether the insurance granted by the merchants is licit or not—it would be difficult to find three who said that this text does not refer to the person who takes for himself more than what he lent for lending and insuring.

- If Gregory IX had wanted to say what is meant by those who hold the second interpretation, he would not have said "because he took upon himself the danger"[19] but "so that he would take upon himself the danger."[20] Those who hold the second interpretation say he refers to the one who lends with the agreement that the borrower will take an insurance from the lender.
- According to the construction and order that the ones who hold the second interpretation give to it, the text refers to the one who insures before lending, because it says "the one who lends because he took upon himself the danger,"[21] and the same people who thus order the text say it refers to the one who lends under agreement that what is lent is insured with him, and consequently they presuppose what he is talking about when the loan precedes the insurance, thus contradicting themselves without realizing it. If anyone were to say that in some newer editions not *suscepit* (past tense) but *suscipit* (present tense) appears, let him look into the old and most of the new editions where *suscepit* appears, and it matters little here, as the same meaning will be found after close scrutiny.

3. Gregory IX does not analyze issues unless they are uncertain, and there is no doubt at all that there is usury in lending to someone under an agreement that forces him to pay not only what he receives but to do something that is convenient to the lender.[22] There is no doubt that this is carried out when the borrower is forced to insure with the lender. One other thing that few notice is that Gregory IX did not say that he was referring to the usurer but to the one presumed to be a usurer, as he does not say "he is a usurer,"[23] but "he is to be thought a usurer,"[24] meaning that it may be possible that before God the person he is talking about may sometimes not be a usurer, but the Church should consider him such, and according to the second interpretation it would have meant that he is a true usurer before God and the people.[25]

According to this interpretation, there may be good reasons to doubt and to arrive at a conclusion that, once heard, everyone will say is the truth. Because the reason for disbelieving (according to everyone's and our opinion) was that no canon text forbade usury, known as nautical or traiecticia,[26] as is practiced when one lends and insures, assuming the dangers of the trip and of getting lost at sea, which is permitted by civil law for much greater reasons than the others because of the danger that the lender takes on.[27] So, it seemed this would also be licit, according to the canons.

The reason why Gregory IX decided the opposite (even though there was disbelief) was not the reason put forth by the gloss (by Panormitanus and the others) but by the need to put an end to veiled or covert usuries carried out as insurances because many, in seeing that canon law forbade usuries in general but did not prohibit nautical ones (and this one seemed licit because of the danger that the lender took on), took to lending by assuming the risk whether there was danger or not and whether what was lent went through sea or land.

Many borrowed saying they did so to carry it for themselves or for others across the sea, or across certain mountains, or beyond the kingdom, and so forth, in order to find someone who would lend them money interested in what they would gain for the feigned insurance. Even others, who really wanted to borrow to go through those places and did not want to insure it, were forced to insure because the lenders did not want to lend without a profit. Because they could not obtain a profit for lending, they wanted to cover it up and conceal it as insurance. This is the reason why Gregory IX ordered that whoever lent money and obtained more for it (even if he insured it) was to be judged a usurer, even if he said that the money he gave and took was on account of the insurance. This was certainly a very prudent ruling because if the nautical usury were allowed to someone who lent with an insurance, then everyone would give and borrow with an insurance—some saying truthfully and some falsely that they were borrowing to carry it by sea or through dangerous lands.

4. By the same ruling, it has been ordered not long ago in these kingdoms and in those of Portugal that there shall be no exchange from one city in the kingdom to another because it is presumed that there are veiled usuries, as we will explain later.[28] By this same ruling, it is determined that when someone buys something for a price inferior to what it is worth, under agreement that he will give it back for the same price whenever he feels like it, it should be considered a loan and pawn and not a sale in the external jurisdiction.[29]

Also, not only are the other usuries forbidden today by canon law, but even those known as nautical[30] (as the ones mentioned above, such as Hostiensis,[31] stated), which here nobody contradicts, with which Saliceto[32] agrees, and which saying Ioannes Annanias[33] declares he shares, concluding after them that this text corrects a chapter of civil law.[34]

Yet, if we took into account the second interpretation, we should then declare that nautical usuries are more licit than illicit because this text would not prove them to be illicit, and there is not another in the world that proves them to be so—at least outwardly. Finally, it is compelling to hold that the principle of this most solemn chapter would not insist on attaining an uncertain resolution, which would be useless and superfluous, as there is no student with three years of canon study who doubts that it is usury to lend money to another under the obligation of insuring it with him. Saying this of Gregory IX's text is irreverent and insolent temerity.

5. Fourth, we say that it does not contradict at all the argument that we noted earlier and one day seemed to us impossible to work out, as it seemed to the aforementioned, who moved away from this common interpretation, that is, that from our common understanding it follows that whoever insures merchandise that will pass through dangerous places is a usurer if he takes something for it. This practice goes against all of Christianity's customs, against a law[35] that sets a price for insuring, and against the general opinion.[36]

We say that it does not contradict this argument because we deny that from this reasoning that follows. The only reasoning that originated from the first interpretation is that whoever lends money and takes more than what he lent (even if he insures it) must be considered a usurer. Our interpretation differs from what the argument implies in three aspects:

1. It does not include the person who insures without lending, and the other does.
2. It does not include the person who lends something that is not money, and the other does.
3. Stating that the usurer is the one who lends money and takes more than what he lends, even if he insures, is not stating that that person is a usurer but that he should be presumed a usurer, and holding the other view is saying that he is a usurer.

If you should reply with what Saint Antonino stated—that someone who helps others by lending should not be judged as a more inferior human being than someone who does not lend, and, thus, there is no reason why he should not insure and receive something for insuring as much as another—we answer, conceding that before God and in one's own conscience (where only truth is seen and the penitent is believed), that it is licit for the lender and insurer to take an amount of money for the insurance, as much as another who does not lend but insures. However, in the external jurisdiction, he is worse off, presuming that the insurance is carried out to cover and conceal the usury and to hide under goodness what in truth means that he is taking more for lending than for insuring. Because of this,

Gregory did not say here that he is a usurer but that he should be presumed a usurer. This was also Adrian VI's[37] opinion (if I am not mistaken).

All this means that a merchant who sells a piece of cloth on credit for the fair highest price to someone who later sells it for less to the same merchant, who thus pays less money for it by giving a fair lower price, does not commit usury or sin before God, but he would easily be presumed a usurer before men for what we explained in the *Manual*.[38] This would be so even if in selling it on credit for a fair price he did more good than another who did not sell it. Accordingly, if someone else who neither sold it to the original buyer nor did him any good bought it from him, even for a lower price than what the merchant bought it from him, the other buyer would neither be, nor presumed to be, a usurer.

The tutor and guardian cannot buy[39] anything from their subordinates, just as neither the other authorities nor the temporal judges can buy those things belonging to their subjects.[40] Even though they do more good than others who do not buy, they are legally in a worse-off condition than the rest, in order to avoid frauds, at least in the external jurisdiction.

6. The fifth thing we state is that from all this we conclude that if the penitent confesses that he lent money to someone who wanted to insure it to carry it across the sea or through other dangerous places, and with no other agreement or force he insured it for what others would insure it, the penitent should not be forced to restitute anything. However, if he were to confess that he took a larger amount for having lent the money or an amount for having lent the money with the insurance, he should restitute the part he took for the loan. This would also be so if he did not want to lend unless the money was insured with another with whom he shared the profit, as this same chapter proves according to the second interpretation, which, as far as these issues are concerned, is judged to be true.

Another conclusion is that this text does not refer to the person who lends and insures other merchandise. One reason is because it only refers to the person lending money, as the pope used the Latin word *pecunia*, which, even if in its general sense means money and any other goods,[41] according to the particular sense it means only money.[42] In order to indicate that he was using the particular meaning in this chapter, the pope did not leave it alone but added some words to it, saying, "a certain quantity of money,"[43] meaning that he only wanted to apply this rule to those lending an amount of money and not to those lending other goods.

Also, this text—which is far-reaching and deviates from the right road inasmuch as it proposes a new interpretation (they call it *iuris et de iure*) whose opposite cannot be proved[44] (that the person who lends and insures and takes more than what he lent is presumed to take it for lending and thus should be considered a usurer)—should be narrowed[45] and not broadened.

It should also be narrowed because the same reason cannot be found for the one who lends money as for the one who lends other things. This is generally because these other things are appraised, sold, and not lent. This is partly because it is difficult to do as much fraud with goods as with money because there are few to whom they can be given and few who can take them and do fraud without shameful defamation. Only the dealers (and not all of them but only those who deal at sea or in different kingdoms) can take hold of them without it seeming to be fraud. Yet money can be taken by all sorts of people, pretending they will send it to Flanders or out of the kingdom for relatives, friends, business, or their own or someone else's fortune. There is no reason why anyone would commit fraud with these other goods because if an unfair profit is wanted, they can increase their price.

7. The sixth issue is that which we said earlier should be interpreted as follows: nautical usuries are forbidden today by the canon law in this distinct text. It should be understood that they are completely forbidden in the external jurisdiction, if they are carried out for a loan of money, and also in one's own conscience, if and as long as they are carried out for lending money or any other thing. This does not hold true as long as they are carried out only for insuring, providing one charges what another charges only for insuring, which is a new and extraordinary resolution.

Against Molinaeus,[46] this most extraordinary text, which we again praise, declares that it is not only a sin to lend with usury to the needy who take it to sustain themselves but also to lend to the rich and merchants who use it to make a bigger profit, because it is evident that those who borrow to take it across the sea or to fairs are not usually poor people who borrow to support themselves. Concerning this, Gregory IX says that not even with these can those who lend money carry out usury, even if they insure it.

It follows, too, that the guarantor may collect something for guaranteeing, because he does not lend money and does what the insurer does, although the insurer collects from the lender, and the guarantor collects what is owed to him from the person representing the risk or borrower.

Even if Laurencio[47] is not too sure of this judgment, there is nothing to worry about—except when there is fraud. There is such fraud if I did not want to lend you any money unless you take a certain person as the guarantor, with whom I have agreed that he take from you a certain amount that we will divide by two or that he transfer the amount to me, thus releasing himself from the guaranty. There is also fraud if I did not want to lend to you without a profit, and then I send my brother or someone else to whom I have sent money so that he lends it to you under agreement that you take me for guarantor, but then I do not want to be the guarantor if you do not pay me an amount, etc.

8. It is true what Ioannes Annanias[48] says that exchanges are illicit because to give in Rome 100 hard-and-fast *ducats* in the way they are given here is a manner of insurance. All exchanges should not be considered illicit because of some that are illicit. Therefore, it is very difficult to set apart these from the licit ones[49] about which we have not said anything either in the *Manual* or anywhere else. We will now work with the desired[50] assistance in the beginning of the other *Commentary*, trying to be as resolute and brief as in the others, adding: (1) what exchanging is, (2) how it is divided, and (3) what types are licit.

Notes

1. Ed. note: A legal presumption that does not admit contrary proof.
2. Hostiensis, *Summa super titulis Decretalium*; Ioannis Andreae, *In Decretalium Novella commentaria*; Panormitanus, *Panormitani prima in primum quintum Decretalium*, et communis.
3. *eo quod periculum in se suscepit*
4. *recepturus*
5. *Mutuans certam pecuniae quantitatem naviganti, vel eunti ad nundinas recepturus aliquid ultra sortem, eo quod suscepit in se periculum, usurarius est censendus.*
6. Ed. note: Nicolò de' Tudeschi (1386–1445), also known as "abbas modernus" or "recentior," or "abbas Panormitanus" or "Siculus," was a Benedictine canonist. In 1400 he entered the Order of Saint Benedict; he was sent to the University of Bologna to study under Zabarella; in 1411 he became a doctor of canon law, and taught successively at Parma (1412–18), Siena (1419–30), and Bologna (1431–32). Meanwhile in 1425, he was made abbot of the monastery of Maniacio, near Massina, whence his title "abbas." In 1434 he placed himself at the service of Alfonso of Castile, King of Sicily, obtaining the See of Palermo in 1435, whence his name "Panormitanus." During the troubles that plagued the pontificate of Eugene IV, Nicolò at first followed the party of the pontiff but subsequently allied himself with the papal contender Felix V who, in 1440, named him cardinal. In his *Tractatus de concilio Basileensi* he upheld the doctrine of the superiority of a general council to the pope. It was his canonical works, especially his commentary on the decretals of Pope Gregory IX that won him the title of *lucerna juris* ("lamp of the law") and ensured his great authority; he also wrote *Consilia, Quaestiones, Repetitiones, Disputationes, disceptationes et allegationes*, and *Flores utriusque juris* (*CE*, s.v. "Nicolò de' Tudeschi").

7. *eo quod periculum in se suscepit*

8. *mutuans*

9. *Mutuans certam pecuniae quantitatem, eo quod periculum in se suscepit, naviganti, vel eunti ad nundinas recepturus aliquid ultra sortem, usurarious est censendus.*

10. John Major, *In quartum sententiarum quaestiones utilissimae*, dist. 15, quaest. 31, sub fine.

11. Silvestre de Prierias, *Sylvestrina suma, qua summa summarum merito nuncupatur*, verbo *usura*, 3, quaest. 35.

12. Tomás de Vio Cajetan, *Summa Caietani*, verbo usura exterior.

13. Juan de Medina, *Codex de Restitutione et Contractibus*, tit. De usura restituenda, in principio [fol. 144] et postea in versic. Inde, fol. 145.

14. Domingo de Soto, *De iustitia et iure, libri decem*, lib. 6, quaest. 7, art. 1.

15. Lex Periculi pretium, ff. De náutico foenore [Dig. 22.2.5].

16. Laurencio de Rodulfo, *Tractatus de usuris*, in c. Consuluit [*Dec. Greg.*, 5.19.10], part. 3, quaest. 1, no. 8; Antonino, *Summa theologicae*, part. 2, tit. 1, cap. 7, s. 21; and Ioannes Annanias, *Commentaria super prima et secunda parte libri V Decretalium*, [De usuris Rubrica: *Dec. Greg.*, 5.19.19,] no. 37.

17. Panormitanus, Ioannes Annanias, Petrus Ravena, nam Ioannem Andream ob brevitatem non sumam.

18. Argumentum ab illo loco: Si quid minus videtur inesse, inest, et id quod magis, et cetera. c. cum in cunctis, De electione: Authentico multo magis, c. De sacrosanctis [Cod. 1.2.14]. Et qui de uno dicit causa exempli, non negat de alio iuxta leg. Damni infesti stipulatio, ff. De damno infecto [Dig. 39.2.18], et glossam putatam singularem, cap. 1, Ne clerici vel monachi [*Dec. Greg.*, 3.50.1]. Et qui de uno dicit, non negat de alio simili, neque e contrario, ut tradit Dom. in c. Qualis, 25 dist. [*Dec. Grat.*, 1.25.4].

19. *eo quod suscepit in se periculum*

20. *ut susciperet in se periculum*

21. *mutuans eo quod suscepit in se periculum*

22. Argumentum, c. 1, 14, q. 3 [*Dec. Grat.*, 2.14.3.1] et eorum quae ibi latius commenti sumus supra commetario proximo *Comentario Resolutorio de Usuras* sobre el capítulo primero, 14, q. 3.

23. *usurarius est*

24. *usurarius est censendus*

25. Quod veritatem sonat, sicut et verbum *censendus* fictionem, aut praesumptionem, iuxta notata per Bartolum et Iosonem in lege Si is qui pro emptore, ff. De usucapionibus [Dig. 41.3.15].

26. Ed. note: *trajecticius contractus*: the insurance taken from the insurer for the money that is to be taken across the sea.

27. Quod est quid aestimabile, leg. Periculi praetium, ff. De náutico foenore [Dig. 22.2.5].

28. See section 30 below.

29. Iuxta glossam singularem, c. Conquestus, De usuris [*Dec. Greg.*, 5.19.8] quam communiter receptam dixit Antonino Burgensis in capite Ad nostram [*Dec. Greg.*, 5.17.3] col. 15, De emptione et venditione, et esse in usu ait Cassiodorus in decissione 1, De usuris.

30. Ff. et C. de nautico foenore [Dig. 22.2.5; Cod. 4.33].

31. Super hoc ipso capite [*Dec. Greg.*, 5.19.19], per eius textum [De usuris Rubrica, cap. 19].

32. In Authentico, Ad haec, C. de usuris, col. 3.

33. In praesenti [De usuris Rubrica, c. Naviganti], no. 3 citans Petrum ab Ancharano in lege Si, C. De náutico foenore [Cod. 4.33] reprobantem Iacobum Butrigam, qui contrarium tenuit in lege 1 Codicis de náutico foenore.

34. F. tit. De náutico foenore [Dig. 22.2].

35. Lex Periculi pretium, ff. De náutico foenore [Dig. 22.2.5].

36. As related above in section 2.

37. Adrian VI, *In quartum sententiarum*, De restitutione, in quaestione quae incipit occurunt.

38. Martín de Azpilcueta, *Manual de confesores y penitentes*, cap. 17, no. 242.

39. Lex cum ipse, c. De contrahenda emptione, et lex si in emptione, si. ff. eodem [Cod. 4.38.5; Dig. 18.1.34.6].

40. Lex 1, C. de Contractibus iudicum, et legibus Principalibus, c. si certum petatur [Cod. 1.53.1; 4.4].

41. C. Totum, 1, quaest. 3, Lex Quisquis, de legatis fideicommissis 3 [*Dec. Grat.*, 2.3.6; Dig. 32.3.5].

42. Azpilcueta, *Comentario Resolutorio de Usuras*, cap. 1, 2 and 3, 14, quaest. 3 [*Dec. Grat.*, 2.14.3.1–3].

43. *certam pecuniae quantitatem*

44. Iuxta late notata in capite Is qui fidem, de sponsalibus [*Dec. Greg.*, 4.1.30].

45. C. Quae a iure communi, de regulis iuris lib. 6; lex Quod contra ratione, ff. eodem [Dig. 50.17.141].

46. Molinaeus [Charles du Moulin], *Tractatus commerciorum et usurarum, redituumque pecunia constitutorum, and monetarum*, a num. 7 at 11, et a num. 70.

47. Laurencio de Rodulfo, *Tractatus de usuris*, c. Consuluit [*Dec. Greg.*, 5.19.10], part 3, quaest. 31.

48. In praesenti [De usuris Rubrica: *Dec. Greg.*, 5.19.19], no. 46, et sensit glossa unde id hauriunt Baldus et Salicetus in libro 3 Codicis, de exercitatoria [actione Rubrica].

49. Quod testatur Cajetan, *De cambiis*, cap. 1; Medina, *Codex*, fol. 145; Soto, *De iustitia et iure*, lib. 7, quaest. 1, [lib. 6, quaest. 8], et alii alibi.

50. Azpilcueta, *Comentario Resolutorio de Usuras*, cap. 1, 14, quaest. 3 [*Dec. Grat.*, 2.14. 3.1] supra cum hoc commentario excuso.

2

Concept and Types of Exchanges

Summary

9. The eighth thing we add, then, is that exchange, also called *cambium* in Latin, is the changing one thing for another, which the jurisconsults commonly call barter.[1]

The first point is that, strictly speaking, exchanging is not buying[2] or selling or depositing or lending (*mutuum* in Latin). Nor is it what is called *commodatum* ("renting" or "leasing"). It is more of an innominate contract, which in many things differs from those mentioned above.[3]

Second, strictly speaking, exchanging is generally divided into the exchanging of money and the exchanging of other goods. Even if it seems more normal to exchange one natural thing for another natural thing—as when a coin is exchanged for another coin or something else and not as price or money but as a piece of gold, silver, or metal—exchanging can also be considered when one changes coins for coins as long as one is not given for the price of the other but in exchange of it. All things that can be sold can also be exchanged,[4] and money can be sold, as we will see later.[5] This happens every day with coins of different value or metal, as everyone confesses, and even (according to those who study this) with coins of the same metal and value when one is in one land and the other elsewhere. This happens even when they are both in the same place but one is near and the other is not. It also happens when one seems better because it is beautiful, because it is antique, or because of some other reason that motivates the person who wants to obtain it by barter, as every day it is evident that a particular *real*,[6] *ducat*,[7] *doubloon*,[8] or *angelot*[9] may seem lovelier than any of the others.

10. The third issue is that the vernacular language of Spain and the vernacular Latin of some Scholastics today do not use the word *exchange* in as wide a sense as its original meaning. Instead, they use another more frequently. According to the original meaning, every barter is exchange and every exchange is barter. However, the vernacular does not call every barter exchange but only the barter of money for money. It also uses the word *exchange* to refer to many contracts, which are not specifically exchanges but are, rather, buying, renting, and other innominate contracts. So, an exchange (as the vernacular understands it) is every kind of contract of money for money that is not gratuitous, be it a barter, a purchase, a deposit, or anything else. It is also important to differentiate between the Spanish vernacular and the Code of Law,[10] which considers only bartering and permutation as exchange.[11]

Thus, exchanging, as the vernacular understands it, can be divided, according to Saint Antonino[12] (whom the theologians who have later written about the subject have followed), into real exchange and dry exchange. According to them, dry exchange is an imaginary kind of exchange, which in fact is no exchange at all. Laurencio who has also addressed[13] this issue is more accurate when he says that dry exchange is when the exchanger gives before receiving, and it is called dry because he does not receive but gives. According to Cajetan,[14] it can also be divided into clearly fair exchange and clearly unfair and dubious exchange. According to others, it can be divided into pure and impure exchange. Some, such as Medina,[15] call exchanges that do not have elements of other contracts, pure exchange. Soto,[16] however, calls them pure when there is no mixture of unfairness and impure when there is. Yet all these categories are not very useful and are very confusing. That is why it seems more useful to say that there are seven categories, species, or methods of exchange. Hence an exchange may be

1. by profession or work to be offered;[17]
2. for small coinage;[18]
3. by bills of exchange;[19]
4. by true transference;[20]
5. with an interest;[21]
6. by safekeeping; and[22]
7. by buying,[23] bartering, or any other innominate contract.

These categories are easier to understand, and they make the subject broader. This is what the real and dry, the clearly fair and clearly unfair and dubious, and the pure and impure come down to. We will explain each one so that by their motives and rules everyone's questions may be answered.

Notes

1. Lex 1, ff. de contrahenda emptione [Dig. 18.1.1], et lex 1, ff. de rerum permutatione [Dig. 19.3.1] et C. eodem tit. [Cod. 4.38.5; 4.64.1]
2. Ut late declarat dicta lex 1, ff. de contrahenda emptione [Dig. 18.1.1] et lex 1, ff. de rerum permutatione [Dig. 19.3.1].
3. Per leges praedictas, et lex ex placito. C. De rerum permutatione [Cod. 4.64.3].
4. Lex 1, tit. 6, part. 5. Hostiensis, *Summa super titulis Decretalium*, de rerum permutatione, versiculo Quid antem potest permutari.
5. See sections 20 and 32.
6. Ed. note: A Castilian silver coin that was the basis of the Spanish monetary system until the nineteenth century.
7. Ed. note: A gold coin that originated in Venice in the thirteenth century with a weight of 3.60 grams, and which was imitated by different European states. Unit for counting in Castile during the sixteenth and seventeenth centuries. It was equivalent to 375 *maravedis* or 11 Castilian *reales*.
8. Ed. note: Generic name given to the Spanish pieces of 2 gold *escudos*.
9. Ed. note: Spanish version of the French *angelot* (a coin with the image of Saint Michael fighting the dragon with a spear in his two hands on the obverse and a ship on the reverse).
10. Ed. note: *leyes de las partidas*: a medieval code especially written down under Alfonso X the Wise (1252–1284) to unify the legislation. During Alfonso's reign, the kingdom of Castile-León produced a series of lawbooks. The most important were the *Fuero real* (1252–1255) and the *Libro de las leyes* (1256–1258), which, in later redactions, was

known as the *Siete partidas*. The *Fuero real* contained laws for cities, and the *Libro de las leyes* was a collection of territorial laws. It is not clear, to what extent, Alfonso X and his successors played in creating these collections (*DMA*, s.v. "Law Codes: 1000–1500").

11. Tit. 6, part. 5.

12. Antonino, *Summa theologicae*, part. 2, tit. 1, cap. 7, s. 49; Angelica, *Summa Angelica de casibus conscientiae*; Rosella, *Summa de casibus conscientiae*; and Silvestre, *Sylvestrina suma, qua summa summarum merito nuncupatur*.

13. Rodulfo, *Tractatus de usuris*, quaest. 1, part. 3, c. Consuluit [*Dec. Greg.*, 5.19.10].

14. Cajetan, *De cambiis*, cap. 1.

15. Medina, *Codex de Restitutione et Contractibus*, fol. 154.

16. Soto, *De iustitia et iure*, lib. 6, quaest. 8, art. 2.

17. Soto, *De iustitia et iure*, lib. 6, quaest. 8, art. 2, no. 21.

18. Soto, *De iustitia et iure*, lib. 6, quaest. 8, art. 2, no. 19.

19. Soto, *De iustitia et iure*, lib. 6, quaest. 8, art. 2, no. 21.

20. Soto, *De iustitia et iure*, lib. 6, quaest. 8, art. 2, no. 31.

21. Soto, *De iustitia et iure*, lib. 6, quaest. 8, art. 2, no. 34.

22. Soto, *De iustitia et iure*, lib. 6, quaest. 8, art. 2, no. 36.

23. Soto, *De iustitia et iure*, lib. 6, quaest. 8, art. 2, no. 41.

3

The Origin and Functions of Money

Summary

11. Regarding section nine, we state that the exchange or barter of goods that are not money (as was said most correctly by Paul[1] the jurisconsult) is a much earlier operation than buying and selling, which began after money was introduced. Before money came into existence, if someone owned a good and was in need of another, he looked for someone who had it and wanted to exchange it for his possession. This was the case, for example, when someone had wine and wool, but not wheat or shoes, and looked for someone with wheat and shoes who wanted to exchange them for his wine and wool. This is the case even today with some foreigners with whom the Spanish and others deal.

After a time, money was discovered, which was certainly a very necessary discovery on the one hand. On the other, I am not sure whether today it destroys souls because of greed; bodies because of wars, travels, and terrifying pilgrimages; and even itself and the fleets where it travels because of horrifying storms and shipwrecks. The main use and purpose in creating money was as a means of payment in order to buy and sell with it the necessary things for human life,[2] so that it would become a common standard of goods to be sold.[3] After this, coins of a metal or value started being bartered for coins of another metal or another value, such as the thick one for the thin one and the thin one for the thick one. Later, because the currency of a land was worth less there than somewhere else (as today almost all the gold and silver currency from Spain is worth less there than in Flanders and France), the art of exchanging started, which is the art of dealing with currency. By giving and taking one for another, money started getting transferred from where it was worth least to where it was worth most. As happens in our time, many people have increased their fortune by taking *ducats* to Flanders and France in groups of two, four, and ten—some in small barrels, pretending they are olives, and some in wine barrels—and making a big profit with each one. In turn, they brought from those places merchandise that was worth little there but had great value here, thus helping with one but hurting us much with the other.

Aristotle[4] thought it was wrong to exchange and trade with money because he did not think this third use of money was natural or brought any benefit to the republic or had any other purpose but that of profit, which is an end without an end. Saint Thomas[5] said that any art of exchange whose main purpose was only to obtain profit was illicit. Saint Thomas[6] himself, however, declares that the art of exchange is licit if its purpose is a moderate profit to support oneself and one's home and if the art of exchange brings about some benefit to the republic. We say that if it is exercised as it should be and the purpose of the profit is directed to honestly and moderately support oneself and one's home, then it is licit. It is not true that using money to obtain a profit by exchanging it goes against its very nature because, even if it is a different use than the first and main one for which it was created, it is still apt for a less principal and secondary use. This happens, for example, when shoes are used to make a profit, which, although it is a different use than the primary one for which they were created (which was to wear on feet), does not go against their very nature.

12. Money has eight different purposes. The first three are the ones already mentioned.[7] The fourth is to display one's riches,[8] showing it to everyone or putting it in the marketplace where it is dealt with or exchanged. The fifth is to use it as medals and clothing decorations. The sixth use is to cheer with its presence.[9] The seventh use is to cure some illnesses with its broth as, they say,[10] is one of the properties of gold powder. The eighth use is as security for a debt. For these last five purposes, it is possible not only to lend and exchange money but even to rent it out. Thus, money may be given by way of many contracts: by way of price for a purchased good; by way of merchandise sold for another money; by way of innominate contract of barter exchanging it for something else or for money; by way of lending called *mutuum*, when something else is given back and not the same thing; by way of lending called *commodatum*, in order to get back the same thing given; by way of security for what is owed; and by way of rental of a sum so that the same amount that was given is returned after the person who borrows it takes advantage of its use by showing his riches, or enjoying its presence, or using its broth, or giving it as security, and so forth.

It can be taken[11] by as many ways as it can be given. Because the nature of the aforementioned contracts, by which it is possible to give and take money, is diverse, so there are diverse law regulations that determine if and when they are licit or not. If money is given by way of buying and selling, it cannot be given but for what something else is worth.[12] The same goes for when it is given by way of exchange or barter.[13]

If it is given by way of loan or if it is given as security for one's own loan (whether the same or another is given back), neither a small nor a big sum can be charged.[14] If rented out to enliven or honor with its presence or to cure with its broth or to use as security for someone else's debt, an honest rent may be taken[15] because the nature of this contract is not to transfer the ownership but only the appraised use of money according to the amount of time for which it was taken. It is more important to understand what truly happens than what is feigned to happen.[16] Every time one of these contracts is carried out truthfully and another is feigned, one should judge not by the rules of the feigned one but by the rules of the true one. Thus, if the exchanger truly lends his money, he cannot take anything for this operation, even if he feigns he is exchanging it or renting it out.

Notes

1. In lege I, ff. de rerum permutatione [Dig. 19.3.1].
2. Ut praedictus Paulus ait ubi supra [Dig. 19.3.1], et ante ipsum Aristotle I politicorum, cap. 6 [Aristotle, *Politics*, trans. E. Barker (Oxford: Clarendon, 1948), 1.9 = Didot ed., 1:490].
3. Saint Thomas, *De regimine principum*, lib. 2, cap. 13 et omnes recentiores de hac re loquentes, praesertim Ioannes Calderinus hic [*Dec. Greg.*, 5.19.19, de usuris cap. 11], et Laurencio de Rodulfo, *Tractatus de usuris*, in c. Consuluit [*Dec. Greg.*, 5.19.10], pars 2, quaest. 26, aptus ad hoc textus in lege Si ita, ff. de fideiussoribus [Dig. 46.1.42].
4. 1 Político, c. 6 et 7 [Aristotle, *Politics*, 1.9–10 = Didot ed., 1:490–92].
5. Thomas, *Summa theologicae*, II-II, quaest. 77, art. 1, 3, communiter receptus.

6. Thomas, *Summa theologicae*, II-II, quaest. 77, art. 1.
7. De quibus Thomas, *De regimine principum*, lib. 2, cap. 14.
8. Lex s. Finalis [non potest], ff. commodat [Dig. 13.6.3.6].
9. Quod de auro affirmat Thomas, *Summa theologicae*, II-II, quaest. 77, art. 1, ad 1, 3.
10. Thomas, *Summa theologicae*, II-II, quaest. 77, art. 2, 3.
11. Quippe correlativorum eadem est disciplina, lex 1, C. de cupressis, libro 11 [Cod. 11.77.1], quod late explicat Felinus in prooemium, Gregory [episcopus], a col. 1.
12. Cap. Cum causa ibi iusto pretio, de emptione [*Dec. Grat.*, 2.14.4.5].
13. Nam quoad hoc ipse cambiens emptioris loco habetur: lex sciendum, s. Emptorem, ff. de aedilitio edicto [Dig. 21.1.19.5].
14. Per cap. 1 et quaeque ubi n. 1 annotavimus 14, quaest. 3 [*Dec. Grat.*, 2.14.3.1].
15. Toto titulo ff. Et C. Locati et de locato [Dig. 19.2; Cod. 4.65].
16. Cap. Plus valere quod agitur, quam quod simulate concipitur, c. Illo vos, de pignoribus [*Dec. Greg.*, 3.21.4]; c. Ad nostram, de emptione et venditione [*Dec. Greg.*, 3.17.5].

4

Just and Licit Exchange

Summary

13. We go on to add that in order to make buying and selling just activities, it is necessary that what is bought is worth an equal price to what is being paid for it, and, conversely, that the price paid for it is equal to the goods' worth.[1] For any rental to be just, it is necessary that the use of the item that is rented out is worth the price given for it, and, conversely, that the price paid for it corresponds to what it is worth. So, too,[2] in order for the exchange or barter to be just and licit, it is necessary that what one party gives to the other has the same value as what is being received.

From this it follows that if the purchase of a mule worth 100 *ducats* for 80 or 120 is unfair, as is the renting of a house, the use of which is worth 50 *ducats* a year, for 40 or 60, so the barter of a beast that is not worth 6 *ducats* for another worth 10 is not just. Nor is the exchange or barter of 10 *ducats* in *reales* for 12 *tarjas*[3] licit.

The logical outcome of this is that every time the exchangers carry out a true exchange and barter of money for money, they cannot take more than what the money they give is worth for the barter and exchange, and some little thing that is usually offered for bartering one currency for another after it is counted. It may happen though that on some occasion, for other factors that interfere in making it a less pure type of exchange, something may be taken, as we will explain later. If the inequality of bartered things makes illicit the exchange and barter of natural things—among which the barter is more legitimate or at least more natural[4]—more so will the inequality of the bartered things make illicit the barter of money, which being money is something artificial, not created in the first place to exchange one piece of money for another, but as a unit of measure of the value of things[5] that, wherever one went, might be taken in order to buy whatever was needed.

14. No money exchanger may take for himself more than what he otherwise could for giving his money before the other person gives him his, or for waiting to be paid a month or two or more, or until the next fair.[6] Nor can another licitly give the exchanger some money under agreement that in a year, or in three months, or when the next fair takes place, he gets back that money and an added amount, or he gets something done by him that by its very nature is worth money. Whenever more than the principal is given or taken for reason of the time elapsed, or for waiting, or for advancing the payment, it becomes a veiled loan and contains a veiled usury, as we have already said elsewhere.[7] Just as the person who gives a mule today so that another that is worth much more is given to him in three, four, or six months, is a usurer, so also the person who gives some money today so that in three, four, or six months a larger sum is bestowed on him, is a usurer.

It is not necessary to do what some people[8] require, which is that the goods that one will barter or exchange with someone else's must be produced now and belong now to the person who wants to barter them. First, there are no documents or motives that prove this to be necessary. Second, just as it is possible to buy,[9] pawn,[10] promise,[11] and send[12] what is yet to be born, so it is possible to barter in this way, at least the general barter, which in this is the same as the special one.

Silvestre[13] himself confesses that if I want to licitly barter and exchange 10 *ducats* in Lisbon with 10 *ducats* paid here, it is not necessary that when you give me the 10 *ducats* here that I have them in Lisbon. It is sufficient that I can borrow them over there with an interest, or in some other way, when the time comes to give them to you over there.

Also, if I barter with you 100 pounds of oil that I have here for the same amount or more of oil that you give me in Lisbon, it is not necessary that I give them to you at the same time as you have them there. It is enough that you have them when it is time to give them to me. There is no truth in saying that in order for a barter to take place, it is necessary to barter a specific thing for another specific thing. In the first place, even if this is required for the special barter, it is not for the general one. Second, if this were necessary, almost no merchant who took money in Medina to send to Flanders, or the other way around in Flanders to send to Medina, would do a true exchange,[14] as neither one (even if he had a lot of money where he is supposed to give it) hands over those *ducats*, *reales*, or *tostones*.[15]

Although it is true that in order for the barter to be completed on both sides, and neither side to be sorry for having carried it out, it is not only necessary to give the other party what they want but also that both parties have rendered the delivery, for bartering is an innominate contract. It is not necessary for both parties to have rendered the delivery in order for the bartering contract to be valid, for the other contracts that are not innominate are valid before the delivery is made either on both parts or on one side.[16]

Notes

1. C. 1 [*Dec. Greg.*, 3.17.1] et c. Ad nostram [*Dec. Greg.*, 3.17.5], et c. Cum causa, ibi iusto pretio, de emptione [*Dec. Greg.*, 3.17.6].

2. Quia in omnibus commerciis, et contractibus iustitia commutative est servanda: 5 Ethicorum [Aristotle, *Nicomachean Ethics*, trans. M. Ostwald (Indianapolis: Bobbs-Merrill, 1962), 5.2 = Didot ed., 2:55], et tradit Augustinus, *De Trinitate*, lib. 13, cap. 3 [PL 42:1017] sentit Thomas, *Summa theologicae*, II-II, quaest. 58, art. 6 and quaest. 59, art. 2, Exprimit Scotus, *Quaestiones in quattuor libros sententiarum*, dist. 15, quaest. 2, art. 2. Et quia in hoc permutans aut cambians pro emptore vel venditore est, lex sciendum, s. emptorem, ff. de aedilitio edicto [Dig. 21.1.19.5] facit; c. ad quaestiones cum glossa 3, de rerum permutatione [Cod. 4.64.3].

3. Ed. note: Vellum currency worth 2 units, belonging to the duke of Brittany in the fifteenth century, so called for the shield on its reverse

4. See section 11.

5. Lex 1, ff. de rerum permutatione [Dig. 19.3.1].

6. Quod Hostiensis ait esse pessimum genus usurarum in *Summa super titulis Decretalium*, de usuris [Rubrica], s. an aliquo, sub finem: versiculo Quid si quis pecuniam.

7. Azpilcueta, *Comentario Resolutorio de Usuras*, c. 1, 14, quaest. 3 [*Dec. Grat.*, 2.14.3.1], n. 26, et probatur in c. ad nostram, de emptione [*Dec. Greg.*, 3.17.5] et in c. Illo vos, de pignoribus [*Dec. Greg.*, 3.21.4] cum eis annotata.

8. Soto, *De iustitia et iure*, lib. 7, quaest. 5, art. 2. Cf. lib. 6, quaest. 12.2 [fol. 597]; et ante illum Silvestre, *Sylvestrina suma, qua summa summarum merito nuncupatur*, verb. *usura* 4, quaest. 9, quem ipse non citat.

9. Lex Nec emptio, ff. de contrahenda emptione [Dig. 18.1.8].

10. Lex Et quae nondum, ff. de pignoribus [Dig. 20.1.15].

11. Lex Interdum, ff. de verborum obligationibus [Dig. 45.1.73].

12. S. Ea [quoque res] quae, Institutionum, de legatis [Inst. 2.20.7].

13. Silvestre, *Suma*, verb. *usura* 4, quaest. 9, vers. septima.

14. Quod absurdum dictum est ad dicendum: lex Nam quod absurdum, ff. de operas libertorum [Dig. 38.1, Nam absurdum], et cap. Dudum, de praebendis lib. 6 [*Liber Sextus*, 3.4.14].

15. Ed. note: Originally from the mid fifteenth century, the *tostone* was the currency of Milán called the *testoné*. It was the Castilian currency called *real de a ocho* in the seventeenth century.

16. Per late notata in lege Si pecuniam, ff. de condictione causa data [Dig. 12.4.5], et lex Ex placito, C. de rerum permutatione [Cod. 4.64.3].

5

Exchanging as a Profession

Summary

15. There is great doubt as to whether it is licit to practice the first type of exchange as a profession and to work as a lender. Cajetan[2] says he had a few cases where the exchanger, as long as he was a lender who offered to lend to those who needed money, could receive an amount of money for a certain amount lent for a certain period of time (according to the virtuous man's free will) for the work and diligence put into looking for, keeping, and taking care of a large amount of money, which are necessary for carrying all this out and then for keeping account, taking guaranties, and assuming dangers and anxiety. This is what Durando[3] and Medina[4] agree on too. They believe in the first place that the so-called lender does not get anything for lending but for the work he offers to do, which is undeniably great, and it is true that there is no usury when a greater amount than what was lent is taken for another just and different reason from lending.[5] In the second place, they believe that the person who is in charge of exchanging one currency for another that will be paid at a later date, may be given something for that business and work,[6] and the same reason seems to apply in this case.

In the third place, according to Scotus,[7] the republic may establish the existence of a money lender who lends for a certain amount and for a certain period of time. This is licit if it is ordered by the republic. If it is licit, and not forbidden, anyone can borrow from him and take advantage of his service, paying a fair amount for it, according to Scotus[8] himself.

The fourth issue is that the judge, priest, and witness who may not receive anything for their rulings,[9] sacraments, and testimony may receive something for their sustenance and the work they carry out. Fifth, when the exchanger lends to someone, he is prevented from dealing, and thus, he may take for himself an interest for profit as we state in another commentary[10] and below.[11] Sixth, the clergyman may take more for going to say Mass some miles[12] away, or for going today, than if he said it here or by chance.[13] Seventh, as we have seen in another commentary,[14] the Mounts of Piety are licit, and in them the poor people who borrow money are allowed to give a certain amount according to the amount borrowed so that every month there is money to pay for the salary of those carrying the burden of caring for the money, keeping accounts, and standing ready to loan.

16. Others[15] hold the opposite view. They affirm that holding this opinion amounts to saying that the art and business of lending under moderate usuries may be ordered and even be carried out without ordinance. This seems to go against the Gospel's spirit, as well as the natural law and canon law, and against all the interpreters and doctors of them. This they consider sufficient answer to the arguments presented by the counterpart. If the profession is not licit, neither will it be licit to take a salary for it, or for the work needed to carry it out, or for preparing everything that is needed.

Nor can anything be deduced from the profession of judge, witness, ecclesiastic, and chaplain for this, because those are licit, but this is not. That is why it does not follow that if for the responsibility, work, and maintenance of these something must be given, so, too, should something be given for lenders. Additionally, because they hold that the Mounts of Piety are not licit, they do not have to reply to the seventh argument, which seems one of the strongest. Even if we consider that they are licit, there is still a big difference between lending and the Mounts of Piety, because in lending there is a profit that is looked for and wanted, whereas it is not there where only compensation for the one in charge of it is sought so that he does not have to offer gratuitously from his own house his valued work, care, and industriousness. In a loan, the money belongs to the lender, and to him belongs its safekeeping; in the Mounts of Piety the money belongs to the poor or to someone else who gives it to the poor, and the Mounts of Piety are the safekeepers. What they give or pay is very small, and is brought together with a donation or just contribution and according to the profit obtained by the one who takes money. Because of this and other reasons, one may not infer from the Mounts of Piety that it is licit to carry out the art and business of lending under moderate usuries.

The opinion that it is licit to take moderate usuries for the profession of lending sounds more substantial to us than the opponents suggest. First, their opinion is based on assuming as certain what is precisely in doubt. What is in doubt (at least implicitly) is whether that profession is licit. The one viewpoint holds it is licit, but the opponents hold it is not.[16] Also, they do not respond to the first argument: there is no usury when more is not taken than what is given for lending, although something more can be taken for a good and just reason. Soto himself confesses somewhere[17] that one can licitly take a salary when one is forced to lend to the republic every time it is in need.

17. From Soto's opinion[18] what cannot be denied (to our way of thinking) is that the republic might give a certain salary to someone who is required to collect money and to have a certain amount ready to lend to those in need of it once a year and to collect it from someone else to lend it in turn to others. Thus, a person who was forced to do all this would take that salary every year, not essentially for lending, but for being required to have the amount of money to lend and to suffer the above mentioned troubles and worries.

Additionally, it should be established that it is licit and useful for the republic to have someone forced to gratuitously lend a certain amount every year, and it cannot be denied that the republic may give a just salary to the person in charge of that business, as Doctor Scotus's excellent words[19] advocate.

Also, if the business of gratuitously lending to the poor is licit, and if for the licit business the republic may make a salary mandatory, it may order a salary for this business and thus charge a sum from those who take advantage of that business and position. Consequently, it may order that they pay the republic a salary in proportion to their loan or a wage that is part (according to the extent to which they profited) of that salary. Consequently, in order not to waste any time or have extra expenses, those who took advantage of this would pay that amount to the person in that position, depending both on the amount they took and on the length of time for which they borrowed.

Also, the reasons and authority of the Holy See—because of which in another commentary[20] we concluded that the Mounts of Piety were licit, holy, and worthy of praise—conclude that this, too, is licit.

Therefore, if someone may be licitly appointed to be in charge of the exchange for small coinage because it is licit and useful (according to what will be said later), and he may licitly take a salary from the republic or from those who profit from the position according to the profit they gain, as it is actually done, then for the same reason the aforementioned practice will be licit.

18. For these reasons (except the due correction) we bring into agreement both opinions in the following manner: The first determines that the republic set up with its authority the aforementioned profession, and we even dare to hope kings and princes provide their republics with such lenders that are made to do what we said above and are forbidden under heavy penalties to take more than what is determined by your Highnesses. However, the habit of wrongly earning too much money will make it difficult to find someone who wants to earn a just salary.

The second should be applied to the person who assumes the profession of lending without having permission to carry it out by private authority. It does not follow that because the profession is in itself licit that each one may take hold of it with no other authority and take for his sustenance whatever would be reasonable for the republic or for its prince, according to Scotus's[21] excellent presumptions. Consequently, in everything, Durando's[22] and Medina's[23] opinions are correct. So we say that it should not follow. First, because Durando and Medina refer also to the one who has not been allowed to carry out the profession and who has other motives than the one who has permission to do so. This is the main argument behind our belief that this profession is licit and a salary may be taken for it. Also, even if these reasons ever proved that it would be licit before God and in one's own conscience to practice this profession with a holy purpose (even without permission) and to take advantage of it before men and in the external jurisdiction, taking less money than the person forced to practice it, he should be judged a usurer to avoid greater frauds, which would be committed under cover of piety according to what we have said above[24] about the lender and insurer.

Notes

1. Ed. note: The *Mons Pietatis* was a public pawnshop, regularly financed by charitable donations and run not as for profit but for the service of the poor. It charged a small fee for its care of the pawns and for the expenses of administration, including the salaries of its employees, so that the capital would not eventually be exhausted by the costs of the business (See Cajetan, *De monte pietatis*, in *Scripta philosophica*, cap. 1).

2. Cajetan, *De cambiis*, cap. 2.

3. Durando di San Porciano, *In quattuor libros sententiarum*, lib. 3, dist. 27, quaest. 2, licet non asseveret.

4. Medina, *Codex de Restitutione et Contractibus*, fol. 147 [De cambiis et lucro per eadem acquisitio, fol. 155].

5. Quod ex definitione usurae in Azpilcueta, *Comentario Resolutorio de Usuras*, c. 1, 14, quaest. 2 [*Dec. Grat.*, 2.14.3], no. 5 posita colligas [8].

6. Quia est dignus mercenaries mercede sua: Luke 10[:7], c. 1, 13, q. 2 [*Dec. Grat.*, 2.13.2.1].

7. Scotus, *Quaestiones in quattuor libros sententiarum*, lib. 4, dist. 15, quaest. 2 [fol. 93].

8. Scotus, *Quaestiones*, lib. 4, dist. 15, quaest. 2 [fol. 94].

9. C. Non sane, 14, quaest. 5 [*Dec. Grat.*, 2.14.5.15], ubi de iudice et teste: c. Sicut pro certo [*Dec. Greg.*, 5.3.39], et c. nemo, de simonia [*Dec. Greg.*, 5.3.14], ubi de aliis.

10. Azpilcueta, *Comentario Resolutorio de Usuras*, cap. 1, 14, quaest. 3 [*Dec. Grat.*, 2.14.3.1], no. 45.

11. See sections 34 and 35.

12. Ed. note: *dos leguas*: a legua is a unit of distance from about 2.4 to 4.6 statute miles.

13. Innocentius receptus in c. Quoniam, de simonia [*Dec. Greg.*, 5.3.40].

14. Azpilcueta, *Comentario Resolutorio de Usuras*, cap. 1, 14, quaest. 3 [*Dec. Grat.*, 2.14.3.1] a no. 64 usque ad 70.

15. Cajetan, *De cambiis*, cap. 2, quem sequitur Soto nec illo, neque ullo alio relato, libro 7, quaest. 3, art. 11, *De iustitia et iure* [lib. 6, quaest. 10, art. 2, fol. 589].

16. Et ita est petitio principii, aut ratio eadem cum dicto, contra lex 1, adiuncta glossa et Paulo, ff. De exceptione [rei venditae], [Dig. 22.2.1].

17. Soto, *De iustitia et iure*, lib 6, quaest. 1, art. 2, ad. 6 [4 argumentum].

18. Soto, *De iustitia et iure*, lib 6, quaest. 1, art. 2, ad. 6 [4 argumentum].

19. Scotus, *Quaestiones*, lib. 4, dist. 15, quaest. 2, art. 2, s. sequitur [fol. 95].

20. Azpilcueta, *Comentario Resolutorio de Usuras*, cap. 1, 14, quaest. 3 [*Dec. Grat.*, 2.14.3.1], no. 66.

21. Scotus, *Quaestiones*, lib. 4, dist. 15, art. 2 [fol. 95].

22. Durando, *In quattuor libros sententiarum*, lib. 3, dist. 37, quaest. 2.

23. Medina, *Codex*, De rebus restituendis, ad fol. 147 [De cambiis et lucro per eadem acquisitio, fol. 154].

24. See sections 3 and 4.

6

Exchange for Small Coinage*

Summary

Exchanging for small coinage is licit and is useful for the republic. A public officer may be appointed for it, with a salary ... **19**

The difference between his position and the exchanger's ... **19**

Someone may be in charge of exchanging, and not be a public officer ... **19**

Money may be exchanged according to its intrinsic value, even if it is not worth that amount by law ... **20**

Money that is appreciated by law is worth more for its exceptional utility ... **20**

Exchanging for small coinage is illicit in certain circumstances ... **20**

19. According to everyone,[1] it is licit to exchange for small coinage, which is exchanging large for small currency and small for large, such as 1 *ducat* for 11 *reales* or 375 *maravedis*, or the other way around, exchanging 11 *reales* or 375 *maravedis* for 1 *ducat*. Because the republic would benefit greatly from having a public officer in this position, it may order a just salary to that person.[2] The republic would take his payment from the public income or order that those who make use of the service of exchanging or bartering hand over a percentage to him. As it is ordered in these kingdoms,[3] for the exchange of 1 *Castilian*,[4] 4 *maravedis* may be taken; and for the *ducat* and *dobla*,[5] 3; and for the *florin*,[6] 2.

According to the law of these regions,[7] this position may go to any exchanger as by its name, too, it is suggested. The law, though, establishes a difference between the public officer and the exchanger. The exchanger's job is to weigh[8] all currency in gold and silver, to say what each is worth, and to settle the amount between the parties who are taking and giving the money. In Seville, this person may neither be an exchanger, nor have any money to barter, nor take any remuneration for weighing it. Instead, he should own a house, scales, and receive a salary from the republic.[9] There was a person who was employed in both positions (I do not know what his fee was) in this very renowned Salamanca in those very rich days of gold and when I was university professor in canon law. The exchanger, for the trade of a 24-carat gold *doubloon* took 2 *maravedis* that remained from the 22 *reales*, and for 22 *reales* and 4 *maravedis* he gave a *doubloon* from those same ones.

Cajetan says[10] that no person who is not in that public position may take this excess licitly. We disagree, as do Medina and Soto for their own reasons because of the trouble and work that go into this type of barter—going to the chamber, opening the safe box, counting once and again, and putting the money away, all of which are activities that may be assessed in monetary terms.[11]

However, some say[12] that it is forbidden in these kingdoms for any private individual to take anything more for exchanging small coinage, although we do not think so. In the first place, these people do not claim any law that bans this. Second, the laws that refer to these matters only forbid[13] anyone from taking on the position of exchanger to publicly exercise the business of exchanger without public authorization. And he cannot be a foreigner, even if such a person has acquired the citizenship. Third, the Pragmática[14] clearly states three times that the exchanger and any other person may take an extra amount for making the exchange.

20. However, it might be possible to prohibit—if it were convenient—that the price of money not be altered so much and that the large currency not be taken out of the country. In order for someone to barter his large pieces of money for small ones with a profit, we have seen foreigners in Portugal give to the natives in private much more than what the gold coins were worth in order to take them to another kingdom, thus bringing about great damage to the first one.

We also believe that the person who has some very fine gold coins may sell them or exchange them as coins and pieces of gold. He may take for himself something more of what they are worth (according to what the law establishes) from the person who wants them to gild something, or to use it for medicines and other things, as long as they are really worth more because of what they are made of, or, if by giving them, he loses the advantages he was enjoying that are worth the same or more than what is being paid in excess.[15]

This was a frequent practice in Toulouse, France, in our time, whereby those who had the gold coins sold them for gilding to the knife owners, who bought the *cruzados*[16] in Portugal (no longer found there) at an even higher price than the *ducats* with two faces from these kingdoms, which no longer appear on them. Medina[17] does not agree with this and goes against the norm without a good solid reason for doing it. Our opinion (also held by Soto)[18] is based on the fact that even if the republic has increased the value of that coin in a certain amount for its principal use (that of being a price for things), and if no one can sell wheat (justly appreciated) for more than that fixed price, and if nobody can be forced to give the money for more than what it is appraised, there are other uses for it for other particular reasons, which the law calls exceptional utility.[19] The one who owns the coins may take an extra amount from the one to whom he gives them.[20]

However, this exchange, which in itself is the most natural of all, may turn illicit if the exchanger takes more for himself than what is owed to him according to just law or custom; if he gives false money, a mistaken percentage, or is delayed in giving his part to the person who is requiring the exchange; if he is deceiving as far as the value of the gold piece is concerned when the one who barters ignores what the Pragmática in these kingdoms[21] has determined; and, finally, if the person who receives the exchange does not pay the exchanger what is owed to him.[22]

Notes

* Ed. note: *cambio por menudo*: the small coinage for exchanging is created to substitute for the large money for amassing.

1. Laurencio de Rodulfo, *Tractatus de usuris*, in c. Consuluit, de usuris [*Dec. Greg.*, 5.19.10]; Antoninus, *Summa theologicae*, 2 parte, tit. 1, cap. 7, s. 47. Quibus etiam Cajetan, Medina, et Soto accedunt.

2. Iuxta singularem theoriam Scotus, *Quaestiones in quattuor libros sententiarum*, lib. 4, dist. 15, quaest. 2 [fol. 95].

3. Pragmática, 129.

4. Ed. note: A gold coin from Castile coined by Henry IV since 1471 with a castle on its obverse. In 1483, it was the equivalent to 485 *maravedis*. In the sixteenth century, the gold *Castilian* belonging to the Catholic Sovereigns was in use. It was carved in Seville in 1475 and weighed 4.60 grams. On the obverse the busts of the Catholic Sovereigns faced each other and on the reverse were the arms of Castile and León.

5. Ed. note: The name given by the Christians to the *almohade* piece of gold, which doubled the weight of the *dinar* of 2.35 grams. The system lasted until the fall of the Granadine kingdom. In general it doubles any gold coin.

6. Ed. note: Originally a gold coin from Florence; imitated principally in Aragón. In Castile in 1454 it was the equivalent to 50 *maravedis*.

7. Praedicta pragmática, 129.

8. Pragmática 126 et 127 in libro pragmaticarum.

9. Pragmática, 125.

10. Cajetan, *De cambiis*, cap. 1 and 6.

11. Quidquid aliqui praedictorum dicant. Non enim officium fuit causa recipiendi illud plus, sed potuisse plus aliquid recipi propter operam, et impedimenta fuit causa instituendi officium, et quamvis uterque laboret in numerando, gratia tamen eius, qui cambium petit, uterque labor principaliter sumitur.

12. Soto, *De iustitia et iure*, lib. 6, quaest. 12, art. 1 [fol. 591].

13. Pragmática, 123.

14. Pragmática, 129.

15. Argumentum eorum qui in Azpilcueta, *Comentario Resolutorio de Usuras*, cap. 1, 14, quaest. 3 [*Dec. Grat.*, 2.14.3.1], n. 45 diximus post Thomam, *Summa theologicae*, II-II, quaest. 77, art. 1.

16. Ed. note: A Portuguese coin called *cruzado de ouro*. The Portuguese *cruzado* was worth 375 *maravedis* in Castile.

17. Medina, *Codex de Restitutione et Contractibus*, De pecunia an vendi possit, fol. 157.

18. Soto, *De iustitia et iure*, lib. 6 quaest. 12, art. 1 [fol. 591].

19. Glossa Bartholi, Baldi, Decii, et aliorum in lege I, C. de sententiis quae pro eo quod interest proferuntur [Cod. 7.47.1].

20. Argumentum lex Si in emptionem, ff. de non numerata pecunia [Dig. 22.77.1] et eius quod ait Thomas, *Summa theologicae*, II-II, quaest. 77, art. 1.

21. Pragmática 126 et 127, et melius 129, et quia in altero plus iusto recipit, in altero dat minus.

22. Quamuis aequalitas est servanda: 5, *Ethica* [Aristotle, *Nicomachean Ethics*, trans. M. Ostwald (Indianapolis: Bobbs-Merrill, 1962), 5.2 = Didot ed., 2:56], et supra no. 13.

7

Exchanging for Bills of Exchange

Summary

21. It is also licit, according to everyone, to practice the third type of exchange, which is to exchange for bills of exchange. This is a virtual transference of money by which someone who wants an amount of money in another land gives it in this land or does something that is worth that amount, or partly does and partly gives to the exchanger or to anyone else who has money or credit in the other place. He then receives bills of exchange for which an amount of money is given to him over there that is equal to the amount he gave or what he did here. He will also give a sum as profit for arranging that the money be given over there in exchange for the bills of exchange.

This is called "exchange for bills of exchange" because it is usually carried out with these certificates, although it is also practiced through a messenger or the person himself who goes to that other place and gives the amount.

This contract is just and much praised by Baldo,[1] although he does not give a special name to it, and we do not believe it has one, because it greatly conforms to Calderini's opinion[2] and to the opinions of the wisest jurists. However, if we had to come up with a name for this type of exchange, it would be that of a purchase or sale agreement; exchange or barter; loan or rent of work, labor, industry; and credit to or from another in order to hand over the money where it is needed. However, it is none of these properly and purely. First, none of the substantial things of any of these is completely or by itself included in this type of exchange of which we are speaking. Second, out of one hundred people who exchange in this way, there are not four who think they are buying or selling, lending or borrowing money, bartering, or renting work and labor from the exchanger in order to receive it someplace else. Contracts, after all, depend on the contracting parties' intentions.[3]

22. If it were any of the aforementioned kinds of contracts, it would be that of a contract renting the work and industry of transferring something from one place to another from another person. This, however, is not so. In this case, the ownership of the thing to be transferred[4] is not passed on to the person who is to transfer it, but in an exchange for bills of exchange, it is; the ownership of the money that is to be transferred and is given to the exchanger is bestowed on him. However, it is the kind of contract that does not have a special name, which the jurisconsults call[5] innominate. It can consist of (1) giving so that you give to me, (2) giving so that you do something for me, and (3) giving so that you give and do[6] something for me. In other cases, (1) I do in order that you give or do, or (2) I do and give in order that you give and do, and so forth. I give you the money here so that you give me bills of exchange or you do something so that others will give them to me, or you yourself give me the same amount of money in that other place, for which I pay you a just salary on account of your work,[7] industry, and credit, which you have already offered and now will offer again and make others offer so that I receive in that other place.

23. When contracts with a special name differ in other things from contracts without a specific name,[8] they do agree with them in that in order for both types of contract to be just, they also require that what is given or done by one of the parties is worth as much as what is given or done by the other party. According to Scotus's solemn rule,[9] in every contract that is properly such where one party gives to another and there is not an intention to do it for free, there must be equality between what one party gives or does and what the other gives or does. Consequently, in order for this contract to be licit, it is necessary to give a just salary to the exchanger for conferring a document that makes someone else give money to its holder in another place, and it is necessary that he not take more than what is due.[10] In order to know which salary is just and which one is unjust for being too great or too small, one must appeal to the law, and if there is none, then one must appeal to custom, if there is one. If both are lacking, then one must appeal to the good and prudent man's free will.[11]

24. Consequently, in the first place, unjust exchanges that are mortally evil are those where the exchanger takes more than his fair salary, even if he sells on credit to the person who does not have any money and will give it back at a later date. The more he takes for having to wait for longer periods of repayment, the worse these exchanges are. Also unjust and evil are those exchanges where the exchanger takes more than his fair salary if he orders that the money be given right away in that other place where it is required, even if the exchanger is satisfied with the one who enters the exchange for having the money returned three or four months later.

Those exchanges are also unjust and mortally evil where, conversely, those who give the money a year or half a year before do it under agreement that the exchanger will not take a fair salary later for giving it to them over there. We see many religious and wise men making mistakes on this issue, and there is proof of such contracts. In all these cases, either the just salary is not paid, or too much is paid, or for giving or taking the money sooner or later more or less is taken from the just price. The reason they are wrong is because of the already[12] stated rule: all contracts that are unequal are unjust. This is also true because of another stated[13] rule in this commentary as well as in another:[14] all contracts where more than the highest fair price is taken in ready money, or less than the lowest fair price is taken in ready money, are formally or visually usurious.

25. In the second place, there is another type of exchange which, according to everyone, is evil and, according to Cajetan,[15] is especially unjust. It is those exchanges that we see every day carried out with kings, noblemen, dealers, and others who take money from the exchangers and give them documents so that they are paid in Rome, Lisbon, León, Flanders, Venice, or other places in a certain amount of time or at a certain fair. Both parties know that the person who is taking it does not have, in that other place, the money, credit, agent, nor intention to pay over there but rather to do so here, where they take it for the price that it is worth in that other fair for which they supposedly took it. The exchanges are worse if the person who takes the money here promises to pay for the exchange in the other place, and then for a new exchange back here if the documents are not valid over there, whereupon the exchanger sends his documents over there, and they return back here notified to whom they are sent with their response that they ignore who is sending the documents, or that they do not want to fulfill their obligations. In the first type of these two exchanges a usury is paid; in the second, two usuries are paid.

26. Also illicit are the exchanges where someone gives money to another party who promises to pay when the fairs of Flanders or of someplace else take place at the rate of what the money is worth there. Carrying out these types of exchanges, looking for ways to deceive God, and showing unfaithfulness is forgetting or not remembering that the divine wisdom sees all our acts with our good and bad thoughts much more clearly than we ourselves. Only in one of these types of the three exchanges can the person be saved from mortal sin and the obligation to restitute. That is when the exchanger finds someone who wants to take his money for a true exchange, and, because he wants to help someone else, he does not give the money to the first person, thus depriving himself from gaining for the just exchange as much as he gains for reasons of the feigned[16] exchange. The reason being is that it is not for his own personal gain.[17]

27. It is worth noting that even if there is a statute where the documents of exchange are naturally enforceable, the documents of feigned exchanges are not, as Annanias[18] said it was stated in Bononia. If instead the exchange contained in the document were partly true and partly feigned, only the part that is real could be enforced, and the adversary would have to confess what was true regarding the document.[19]

In the third place, it is also illicit if I give you 1000 *ducats* right now under agreement that you will have them given to me in Rome in a year's time, unchanged in their amount, for the advantage you took of them in the time you had them. It is usury on my part if for giving the payment in advance I earn the salary that I should have given you if you had had them given to me immediately.[20]

28. In the fourth place, even if Doctor Soto[21] determined in some text that nothing could be taken for this type of exchange when the bills of exchange were given in one city of the kingdom for another in the same kingdom—such as from Medina to Toledo or Seville—in another part of his work[22] he approved and said it was allowed. Soto had two reasons. First, the reasons we talked about earlier that justify this contract from here to Rome also justify the contract from here to León, and from here to Pamplona, Burgos, Seville, and Toledo, as long as the exchange is carried out sincerely and without fraud and as long as one takes less when there is a shorter distance and fewer dangers, work, and coastlines involved through which to pass, take, keep, and safeguard the money than when more distant places are involved. Second, the argument that holds that documents for another kingdom that are feigned usuries are illicit, concludes, on the contrary, that documents that are destined to another city in this kingdom are licit if they are genuinely, without fraud or deception, given for an honest salary.

Some say, however, that exchanges from one part of the kingdom to another are banned by new prohibitions both here and in Portugal because these were generally carried out to cover usuries. However, we consider that they should be limited and not be banned if the exchanger receives before giving or having someone else give. The first reason is that it is difficult to feign usury when the exchanger receives before giving, which receiving is common with this type of exchange. Usuries are feigned when it is the other way around and the exchanger gives first and receives later, a type of exchange that the Bononienses call dry, as was said earlier,[23] invoking Laurencio.[24]

The second reason is that this type of exchange has a law unto itself and respects the divine, canon, and civil law; and laws should not be changed unless the usefulness and goodness sought after are evident.[25] This does not seem to be the case with this prohibition. Moreover, if it were banned, students, pilgrims, and many other dealers would be bereft of a good way to transfer (almost without expenses and danger) the supplies and money from Seville and other similar cities to Salamanca, Burgos, and other parts; and from Burgos and other such cities to Seville and other far away places between which there are dangerous roads.

29. However, there is great cause to forbid the exchange within the kingdom when the exchanger gives in advance in order to receive more either now or at another time. This exchange should be forbidden because it is probable that many usuries would be concealed by this type of exchange. To my weak understanding, however, there is little usefulness in this, because it does not remove the instruments that veil profit from the usurers who want to go ahead with veiled exchanges. In fact, it gives them the opportunity to do what they did before with fear and shame and less profit for one of the kingdom's cities, now without fear and with much more profit for another city outside the kingdom. It would be a much better solution to have honest judges examine the past and present exchanges and, if they were to find from the people's situations that they are veiled, punish those who did them for wherever it was, carrying out the old laws that have not been revoked by this new ban,[26] which is not contrary to them.

Another reason why there is little usefulness in forbidding this type of exchange is because it conceals and almost forgives past actions, which is an unjust mercy,[27] because, when past actions are concealed and future actions are banned, there is opportunity of doing what is banned, in hopes that the actions are once again concealed, and going against clement justice, which by means of punishing past actions stops evil people from committing future ones.[28] However, it makes it easier to learn about the feigned exchanges because it is easier to see that this Spanish person who takes money to pay it in Flanders does not have money there, just as it was possible to see that he does not have it in Seville. Although we have already seen frauds against this in Lisbon, where a gentleman who needed money did not take it himself for Medina but asked a dealer to take it for himself, promising to pay them there with the exchange. So true is what the Italian said: "The law is no sooner made than the fraud ensues."[29]

30. In the fifth place, His Majesty's past intention to prevent the disorder caused by taking an exorbitant profit for this type of exchange was a holy one, and he ordered that for the exchange from these kingdoms to Rome no more than 400 *maravedis* per Chamber *ducat*[30] could be taken, and from Rome to here no more than 420. From these kingdoms to Naples one could not take more than 400 per long *ducat*, and for Besançon per the *mark's*[31] *escudo*[32] no more than 375. Neither could one take more than 390 from Besançon to here per *escudo*, nor more than 370 from here to Flanders per *escudo* of six salaries[33] of 60 *maravedis*, nor less than 70 from Flanders to here for *escudo*. Neither could one take more than 380 from here to Valencia per gold *Castilian*, nor more than 510 per a *Castilian* from Valencia to here. Neither could one take more than another *ducat* over there from here to Zaragoza per *escudo*, nor more than 400 from Zaragoza to here. And one could take from here to Barcelona only what has been common, and from here to Portugal per *ducat* no more than 370, which are there worth 400 *reales*, and no more than 385 from Portugal to here per *ducat*.

After this moderating provision, His Royal Majesty forbade exchanges in all of Spain. That is, it was forbidden from the kingdoms of Castile to those of Aragón, Cataluña, and Valencia, and even to those of Castile, with some small limitations that would make the exchanges possible, and those are that the exchanger must receive the money before giving it, for the reasons already mentioned.[34]

Let us hope everything is carried out with as much watchfulness, integrity, and perseverance as the good intentions that have been displayed. Although I fear this will not be so, at least as far as exchanges are concerned I hope this will be so from the kingdoms where money is worth more and there is more merchandise. Those who have money there will not want to give their money before, so that they are paid less here than what it is worth in those other parts, as we have noted below in the exchange from Flanders and Portugal to here.

Notes

1. In cap. de plus petitionibus [*Dec. Greg.*, 3.3] no. 9 dicens eum esse iustum et iuris gentium.
2. Giovanni Calderini and Gaspar Calderini, *Consilia domini Iohannis Calderini et domini Gasparis eius filii redacta*, con. 11 [De usuris Rubrica].
3. Quia actus agentium non operantur ultra fines eorum: lex Non omnis, ff. de rebus creditis [Dig. 12.1.19] et. Cum super, de officio delegati [*Dec. Greg.*, 1.19.23].
4. Argumentum lex 2, s. finalis, ff. locato et conducto [Dig. 19.1.2]; Inst. De locato, per totum [Inst. 4.65.1–35].
5. Lex Naturalis, ff. de praescriptis [Dig. 19.5.5] adiuncta lex si, [Dig. 19.5.7] cum glossa et ei annotatis, ff. De conditione causa data [Dig. 12.4].
6. Iuxta doctrinam Bartholi in dicta lege Naturalis, s. sed si facio [Dig. 19.5.5.4] sub finem [no. 6].
7. Argumentum: lex Periculi, ff. de nautico foenore [Dig. 22.2.5], et lex Traiectitiae, ff. De actionibus et obligationibus [Dig. 44.7.23] lex Qui Romae, s. 1, ff. De verborum obligationibus [Dig. 45.1.122.1].
8. Iuxta notata in lege Si pecuniam, cum glossa verbi Poenitere, ff. De conditione causa data [Dig. 13.4.5], et lex Ex placito, C. De rerum permutatione [Cod. 4.64.3].
9. Scotus, *Quaestiones in quattuor libros sententiarum*, lib. 4, dist. 15, quaest. 2, art. 2 [fol. 95] quod probatur 5 *Ethica* [*Nicomachean Ethics*, trans. M. Ostwald (Indianapolis: Bobbs-Merrill, 1962), 5.10 = Didot ed., 2:57], et per scripta Thomae, *Summa theologicae*, II-II, quaest. 58, art. 6 et quaest. 59, art. 2.
10. Bartolome Saliceto, *Lectura super IX libris codicis*, in authentico, Ad haec, quaest. 11, De usuris [Rubrica].
11. Argumentum: c. 1, de constitutionibus [*Dec. Grat.*, 1.1.1], et c. consuetudo [*Dec. Grat.*, 1.1.5] et dicta lex 1, ff. de iure deliberandi [Dig. 28.8.1], et c. De causis, de officio [et potestate iudicis] delegati [*Dec. Greg.*, 1.29.4].

12. Azpilcueta, *Comentario Resolutorio de Usuras*, cap. 1, 14 quaest. 3 [*Dec. Grat.*, 2.14.3.1; and sections 26 and 14 in the present work].

13. See section 14.

14. Azpilcueta, *Comentario Resolutorio de Usuras*, cap. 1, 14, quaest. 3 [*Dec. Grat.*, 2.14.3.1], no. 4 cum hoc retro excuso, et tent Thomas, *Summa theologicae*, II-II, quaest. 78, art. 2.

15. Cajetan, *De cambiis*, cap. 1 [fol. 163]. Quod omnium soptime resolvit Silvestre, *Sylvestrina suma, qua summa summarum merito nuncupatur*, verbo *usura* 4, quaest. 9, et cambium siccum secundum omnes.

16. Cajetan, *De cambiis*, cap. 1, fol. 163.

17. Ed. note: See Azpilcueta's discussion in section 34.

18. Annanias, *Commentaria super prima et secunda parte libri V Decretalium*, no. 46 [*Dec. Greg.*, 5.19.10], De usuris [Rubrica].

19. Quod late deducit Laurencio de Rodulfo, *Tractatus de usuris*, in dicto capite Consuluit [*Dec. Greg.*, 5.19.10] 2 parte, quaest., 135.

20. See sections 14 and 24.

21. Soto, *De iustitia et iure*, lib. 7, quaest. 3, art. 2, sub finem, lib. 6, quaest. 10, art. 2 fol. 589.

22. Soto, *De iustitia et iure*, lib. 7, quaest. 6, art. 1. Cf. lib. 6, quaest. 3, art. 1, fol. 60.

23. See section 10.

24. In c. Consuluit [*Dec. Greg.*, 5.19.10], 3 parte, quaest. 1.

25. Lex 2, ff. de constitutionibus principum [Dig. 1.4.2], Thomas, *Summa theologicae*, I-II, quaest. 97, art. 1.

26. Argumentum: Lex Praecipimus, C. de appellationibus [Cod. 7.72.32], et c. 1, de constitutionibus lib. 6.

27. Canon: Est iniusta misericordia, in principio; et in fine ibi: facilitas enim veniae, incentivum tribuit delinqueni [*Dec. Grat.*, 2.23.4.33].

28. C. Factae, 4 dist. Facit [*Dec. Grat.*, 1.4.1]; c. Non putes, cum multis sequentibus, 23, quaest. 5 [*Dec. Grat.*, 2.23.5.36 ss.].

29. *Fata la lege trobata la fraude.* Contra legem Non dubium, C. de legibus [Cod. 1.14.5], et c. Certum, de regulis iuris lib. 6.

30. Ed. note: *Ducado de Camara*: the papal *ducat.* It was a gold coin that weighed and was worth the same as the Venetian *ducat* minted by the Apostolic Camera, from which it received its name.

31. Ed. note: A weighing measure for coins. In Castile it weighed 230.0465 grams for silver. For silver it was divided into 8 ounces; for gold into 50 *Castilians.* The *mark* from the Casa de Moneda was used to weigh officially minted coins.

32. Ed. note: A generic name given in the Middle and Modern Ages to diverse gold and silver coins that had a shield on one of their faces. It was also a *Castilian* gold coin introduced in 1535 as a consequence of the casting of coins for the Tunez army. It was equivalent to 10.68 gold *pesetas.*

33. Ed. note: Created by Charlemagne as a counting unit. The salary for the people from Burgos consisted of 12 vellum money notes carved in Burgos.

34. See section 28.

8

Exchanging by Transference

Summary

31. Everyone agrees that it is licit to practice the fourth type of exchange, by true transference, carried out by buying, bartering, or using another innominate contract to give currency that is worth less in one land than in another because it is not used there—because its metal is not worth as much there as in the other place, or because it is broken, disfigured, dented, worn out, or weightless—and to take it to the other land where it is worth more because it is not weighed there or because it is more used there. It can then be exchanged for another currency that is worth more where the other was worth less as long as due equality is maintained. All of this is buying, selling, bartering, or another innominate contract where I give so that you give, as we will see below.[1] All of these are licit if they are equal.[2]

This does not mean that something less was given for one thing in one land, then something more is taken for that same thing in another land. The reason why less is given in one land is because it is worth less there; and the reason why more is taken for it in another land is because it is worth more there. So, what was bought for less in this land may be sold for more in another one; and what was bartered in this land for something of less value, may be bartered somewhere else for something of more value. This applies to all merchandise, as long as much less in one place is not given, and much more is not taken in another such that the just price is dishonored with respect to the prudent man's own free will.

32. Consequently, money may be bought and sold (even though Soto holds the contrary opinion[3]), which is a very true thing when it is not considered as money but as a piece of metal, and as gold, silver, or broken copper. Even when it is considered as money, under any one of the eight aspects, which we will describe below, it can be worth more or less than the price that the law establishes as long as it is offered as merchandise and not as price of other merchandise,[4] if this were to be thoroughly analyzed. Every time that it is considered according to one of these aspects, and not according to the fact that it is the price of other things, it is merchandise that may increase in value more or less and consequently may be bought.[5] The Archdeacon[6] does not hold the contrary opinion, which some try to force on him.[7] Although he ponders it, he does not say that money cannot be sold, but rather that its use cannot be sold inasmuch as it is money without selling money itself. The law[8] determines that everything that may be exchanged may be sold and everything that may be sold may be exchanged, excepting spiritual things, which may be exchanged but not sold. Everyone confesses that money may be exchanged.

33. It follows, too, that this type of exchange would be unjust if for example what is worth less is a piece of land, and the exchanger buys it or exchanges it for even less than what it is worth, and that which is worth more he buys or exchanges for even more than what it is worth, especially when this is done for advancing the price or selling on credit. This principle may be easily proven by the two rules mentioned above.[9] It would also be unjust if money that is forbidden is transferred in such a way that to the others it is unjust to transfer it.[10]

Notes

1. See section 41.
2. Toto titulo: de contrahenda emptione [Dig. 18.1], et de rerum permutatione [Dig. 19.4], et lex 1, cum quatuor sequentibus, ff. De praescriptis verbis [Dig. 19.5.1–5].
3. Soto, *De iustitia et iure*, lib. 7, quaest. 5, art. 3. Cf. lib. 6, quaest. 12, art. 3 [fol. 599].
4. Argumentum: lex 1, ff. de rerum permutatione [Dig. 19.4.1], lex 1, ff. de contrahenda emptione [Dig. 18.1.1], lex 3, s. Si, ff. commodati [Dig. 13.6.3.1]; et eorum quae scripsit Cajetan, *De cambiis*, cap. 6, et Medina, *Codex de Restitutione et Contractibus*, ad fol. 148 [De pecunia an vendi possit, fol. 157]. Quamquam quoad aliqua quae parvi ponderis sunt, dissentire videri possunt.
5. Argumentum: lex 2, ff. Locati [Dig. 19.2.2] et s. Item pretium, institut. De emptione [Inst. 3.24.1.2].
6. Azpilcueta, *Comentario Resolutorio de Usuras*, cap. 1, 14, quaest. 3. Ed. note: "Archdeacon," that is, Gratian. Azpilcueta is discussing Gratian's opinion in *Dec. Grat.*, 2.14.3.1.
7. Ut Laurencio de Rodulfo, *Tractatus de usuris*, in c. Consuluit [*Dec. Greg.*, 5.19.10], parte 2, quaest. 26.
8. Lex 2, tit. 6, partita 5. Hostiensis, *Summa super titulis Decretalium*, de rerum permutatione, v. S. Quid autem.
9. See section 24.
10. Eadem ratione lex illud, ff. ad legem aquilam [Dig. 9.2.32].

9

Exchanging for an Interest

Summary

34. The fifth type of exchange, exchanging for an interest, is also licit. This means that if the exchanger deals with merchandise and for lending to whom it is convenient he stops dealing in exchanges, he may take an interest both for the profit as well as for the loss. As we have proved extensively elsewhere,[1] any merchant may take an interest under certain conditions. We add again that even if he does not deal with other merchandise apart from his exchanges, but if for lending he stops dealing with them (if they are licit), he may take an interest for the profit that for lending he is deprived of earning in his occupation of just exchanger.[2]

Cajetan's[3] aforementioned[4] decision may be applied here, which is the one referring to the person who stops dealing in true exchanges in order to help someone else with a feigned exchange. He may earn what he would earn with the true one. Woe to the one who for this reason does not stop dealing or doing as many true exchanges as before and takes feigned interest without there being a real or probable one,[5] as if God did not exist (who not only sees our acts but even our hearts).

This type of exchange can justify the answer of the doctors of Paris—among whom were those two renowned brothers Antonio Coronel and Luys Coronel (from whose works and advice we used to benefit)—which Doctor Soto[6] criticizes. According to that answer, merchants may take more if they have to wait for their payment until the second fairs than if they wait until the first ones. They can take even more if they wait until the third ones than if they wait until the second ones. Because the exchange of the interest is larger the longer the period, in all probability the person is not earning. It is certain that the dealer who stops dealing and the exchanger who stops exchanging with his money for two fairs is prevented from earning more than if he stopped for one fair, as is the case with the person who does not exchange in two, who is prevented from earning more than the person who does not exchange in one fair. It is hard to believe that such renowned doctors belonging to such a great university had such an understanding of this other type of exchange regarding buying or bartering. Even students with few years of study know that it is usury to buy or barter for a higher price when there is a longer term. This subject, though, is not talked about in schools, according to what Doctor Soto[7] says. It was never discussed until him, although we believe that Gaspar Calderini,[8] Laurencio Rodulfo,[9] Saint Antonino,[10] Ioannes Annanias,[11] Silvestre,[12] Cajetan,[13] Medina,[14] and others studied this subject extensively, even if they did not explain its concepts as much as we did.

35. As far as this exchange is concerned, the exchanger who stops being a merchant to become an exchanger once he has gotten his money out of the deal and devotes all his money to exchange from fair to fair for a certain or uncertain interest, is mortally sinning and must pay restitution. This is the case when he exchanges under agreement that those who take his money will pay him as much as what those who deal in what he used to deal earn, or a certain amount of probable interest that is equal to what he would earn if he were dealing. Because he has already removed his money from the deal and does not want to deal, there is no true or probable interest, as was said in the *Manual*[15] and in another commentary.[16] Also the exchanger sins who in order to exchange his money does not stop dealing with the money he has destined for that purpose. He should pay restitution on what he has earned for the same reason. Therefore, there are many penitents who have enriched themselves in these ways, and many confessors who listen and have listened to them in confession, absolving them without ordering them to stop doing it or to pay restitution on what they have earned, or ordering thus and not being obeyed, which condemns the confessor as well as the penitent.

Notes

1. Azpilcueta, *Comentario Resolutorio de Usuras*, cap. 1, 14, quaest. 3 [*Dec. Grat.*, 2.14.3.1], no. 46 et sequenti, una cum hoc excuso.
2. Quia eadem omnino ratio, idem omnino ius suadet lex illud, ff. Ad legem aquilam [Dig. 9.2.32] et c. Translato, de constitutionibus [*Dec. Greg.*, 1.2.3].
3. Cajetan, *De cambiis*, cap. 1 [fol. 163].
4. See section 26.
5. Quasi non esset Deus, vel non scrutaretur corda, et renes, contra psalmum [25:2]; c. Novit, de indiciis [*Dec. Greg.*, 2.1.13] et c. Deus Omnipotens, 2 quaest. 1 [*Dec. Grat.*, 2.2.1.120].
6. Soto, *De iustitia et iure*, lib. 7, quaest. 5, art. 5. Cf. lib. 6, quaest. 12, art. 5 [fol. 603].
7. Soto, *De iustitia et iure*, lib. 6, quaest. 12, art. 5 [fol. 603].
8. Giovanni Calderini and Gaspar Calderini, *Consilia domini Iohannis Calderini et domini Gasparis eius filii redacta*, con. 11 [De usuris Rubrica].
9. In repetitione c. Consuluit [*Dec. Greg.*, 5.19.10], quaest. 1 secundae partis.
10. Antonino, *Summa theologicae*, 2 parte, tit. 1, quaest. 7, s. 49.
11. In praesenti [De usuris Rubrica c. Naviganti: *Dec. Greg.*, 5.19.10].
12. Silvestre, *Sylvestrina suma, qua summa summarum merito nuncupatur*, verb. *usura*, 4 per totum.
13. Cajetan, *De cambiis*, cap. 1 [fol. 163].
14. Medina, *Codex de Restitutione et Contractibus*, fol. 145 [*De cambiis*, fol. 155].
15. Azpilcueta, *Manual de confesores y penitentes*, cap. 17, no. 212.
16. Azpilcueta, *Comentario Resolutorio de Usuras*, cap. 1, 14, quaest. 3 [*Dec. Grat.*, 2.14.3.1], no. 49.

10

Exchanging by Safekeeping

Summary

36. The sixth type of exchange, by safekeeping, is also just because there is a law,[1] custom, or statute that makes the exchanger a safekeeper, depositary, and guarantor of the money that is given to him or exchanged for something needed by those who give it or send it. This makes the exchanger pay the merchants or the people chosen by the depositors in a particular way, and, because of this, it is licit that they take a just salary from the republic or from the depositing parties, because this profession and work is useful to the republic and does not possess any iniquity whatsoever, "for the laborer is worthy of his hire."[2]

This exchanger's occupation is to receive the money from the merchants; to deposit it; to have it ready; and also to write, keep the books, give an account of the money to everyone, which is very difficult, and run the risk of making a mistake with the accounts and other things. The same thing could be carried out with a contract[3] by which one of the parties commits himself to some people to receive and keep money under deposit, giving, paying, and keeping the books with the people according to the way they tell him, because this is the kind of contract where the activity and work of one is rented out to someone else. Such a contract is specifically provided for by the law and is just and holy.[4]

What the salary should be for this type of work has not been resolved by law. It is worth noting that the exchanger has two ways of taking money: in cash by actually taking the money, and in treasury notes by accepting documents of other exchanges or from other people with which they promise or deposit in his bank the payment of what they remit to him so that he forwards it to his account. There are also two ways in which the exchanger pays: by actually giving the money, or in treasury notes by forwarding the payment to other exchanges.

37. Some[5] believe that it is ordered and established in this kingdom that when the exchanger pays someone in cash, he should receive 5 per every 1,000, and when he pays with a document, remitting to another exchange, he should receive nothing. We have found quite the opposite in the laws of these kingdoms. In one[6] of them, it says that the Catholic Sovereigns ordered, in Seville in the year 1491, that the exchanger could pay those who had treasury notes and others with coins that are defective, broken, and crushed, paying for the defective ones. If someone were to want his payment in sound, healthy, and chosen coins, the exchanger would be able to take 5 per every 1,000 for paying it thus, and not any more, even if the other party wanted to give more.

In another law,[7] it says that the Catholic Sovereigns themselves found out that the exchangers took advantage of such a law to not only take for themselves those 5 per every 1,000 in those situations, but also in all those cases where cash was paid in any coin, whether it was chosen or not. They reviewed that law in 1513, invalidated what pertained to this issue, and established, upon the threat of great penalties, that the exchangers may not pay in broken or crushed money and may not take anything for themselves from those to whom something was deposited in their accounts or who owed them money. This provision was very holy and necessary.

38. It is against all natural, divine, and human reason[8] for you to take from me and others 1, 5, or 10 per 1,000 of what our debtors or others have deposited for us in your bank or exchange, without doing anything else for us than paying what was deposited in your bank. It is unjust[9] that we should pay for your work of taking care of the money from our debtors or from those who deposited with you in our favor or for your work of keeping their accounts. Even if some say there is great effort that deserves the said 5 per 1,000, I do not believe so because it would be unjust unless it is one of the three cases that we will discuss later.

Consequently, not only are the said 5 per 1,000 (when cash is paid) not his salary, but they become his theft and unjust extortion, which drive him either to hell or to restitution and a complete contrition in order to deliver himself from these sins,[10] except in three cases. The first is when the payment goes to the same people who deposited and gave their money in cash for the exchange, and they pay thus to get a discount on the work and care that the exchanger has in receiving and taking care of their money and do it for the aforementioned persons. The second is when the depositors sold their merchandise for a higher price that depended on the higher amount they had to pay for receiving the exchange in cash for the discount and discharge of what the depositors owe the exchanger. The third is when, by their own free will, those who receive the payment give it in order to exchange it for cash so that they do not have to wait for the payment eight or ten days until the payments are due in order to transfer the payment to the exchanger. They do this so that they do not have to leave anything for cashing in, which is something that has happened to us. (Very few people receive the payment and give it to exchange, because the payment is not theirs yet even if the depositors have left it in deposit.) Their will to do this is as unnatural as the will of the one who pays usuries to the usurer, which does not excuse from sin or restitution.[11]

39. Others say that their salary is 2, 3, or 4 percent, according to whether the money belonging to the lenders is more or less expensive or whether they give in cash to some and to others until the next fair. All of this is usury and mortal sin, with the obligation of restitution, and cannot be denied in any way.[12]

That is why we say that the salary is what each dealer gives or should give according to each virtuous man's[13] free will in each fair, once the accounting has been finished according to what is given for it until such conclusion, which is something that is not determined. They tell us that some give them 1 or 1½ per 1,000 apart from what they get for exchanging coins.

If you say that today (when there are no gold pieces to barter) the second amount is little or nothing and the first amount is little to make so many rich, so quickly, and in such a large measure, we will answer that (as is usually said) the exchangers have been a great part of the cause. There are no gold pieces in the kingdom, and they are not bartered, because the exchangers have taken the money out by means of much skill and dexterity, although I believe that there has been a greater cause. We also say that the exchanges were not invented to enrich the exchanger but to make deals more useful and easier so that there is more merchandise and it is cheaper, which would be the case if they carried out their job honestly and would content themselves with a just salary. This just salary would be the result of receiving it from those who owe it to them, whose money they hold and whose accounts they keep and not from those who do not owe it to them, remembering what that great king and prophet said:[14] "It is better to gain little with justice, than many riches with sin." One should also remember that the Author of the prophets said,[15] "What is the use of gaining the whole world, and losing one's soul for it?" and one should not desire, contrary to the Psalm's[16] precept, to imitate the evil ones who gained their riches illicitly.

40. Regarding this type of exchange, not only do the exchangers sin and have to pay restitution but also those who give them money to keep and do what we saw earlier and then do not want to pay anything, saying that what the exchangers earn with their money and receive from those who pay in cash is enough of a salary. Then if the exchangers ask for something, they leave them and go deal with someone else, and so, in order to avoid this, the exchangers decide not to take a salary owed to them but take it from someone who does not owe it to them.

Those who sin, too, are the ones who give the exchangers some money in cash and then, if they take it in treasury notes for themselves or for others and not in cash when the accounts are done with, they make the exchangers offer the payment for having given to them in cash, which is at least at 2 percent. They cannot under any condition take this profit as something owed to them, but for the advantage the exchanger takes or will take from that money that he was paid in cash. Thus it is clearly usury because the exchanger who takes money works in order to receive it, store it, keep accounts, and have it ready for when it is needed or deposited, and the one who gave it or gives it does none of these things.

The exchangers commit another kind of usury regarding this matter when they receive money in cash in their hands, bank, or operating table from a merchant and immediately deposit an additional sum of money in another bank for whatever he wants for as long as they keep his money, and for as long as the merchant leaves with the exchangers the revenue that they would have had to pay because of the cash payment. All this, at least in its intentions, is clearly usury because the dealer leaves the revenue to the exchangers that he thinks he has earned for the cash payment, so that the exchangers lend him by way of deposit another amount, or a sum until the next fairs, and the exchangers lend it so that they do not have to pay that which they owe the depositor. All this is great misfortune and should be grieved over.

Notes

1. Lex Argentarius, s. 1 [Dig. 2.13.10] and Lex Quaesdam, s. Nummularios, ff. de edendo [Dig. 2.13.9.2].
2. *Dignus enim est operarius mercede sua*, Luke 10[:7], et c. 1, 13, quaest. 3 [*Dec. Grat.*, 2.13.1.11].
3. Quia per pactum fieri potest id quod per legem fit: lex Non impossibile, ff. de pactis [Dig. 2.14.50], C. Contractus, cum glossa, de regulis iuris lib. 6 [Dig. 50.17.23].
4. Est enim contractus locationis ex parte campsoris, et conductionis ex parte aliorum, certa mercede constituta, lex 1 et 2, ff. Locati, s. r. Instit. de locatione [Dig. 19.2.1, 2; Inst. 3.15.1].
5. Soto, *De iustitia et iure*, lib. 7, quaest. 4, art. 1. Cf. lib. 6, quaest. 11, art. 1 [fol. 590].
6. Pragmática, 127.
7. Pragmática, 129.

8. Regula: Non debet aliquis alterius odio, praegravari, De regulis iuris, lib. 6; 1 quaest. 4 per totam causam [*Dec. Grat.*, 2.1.4]; c. Si habes, 24 quaest. 3 [*Dec. Grat.*, 2.24.3.1].

9. Argumentum: C. ne filius pro patre [Cod. 4.13], Ne uxor pro marito [Cod. 4.12], per totum.

10. C. Peccatum, de regulis iuris, lib. 6, cum his quae diximus in manuali, c. 17, no. 63 et 64.

11. C. Quia in omnibus, de usuris [*Dec. Greg.*, 5.19.3], c. 1. Eodem titulo li. 6.

12. Per canon 1, 14, quaest. 3 [*Dec. Grat.*, 2.14.3.1], et definitionem usuarae ac alia quae ibidem posuimus; immo est pessimum genus usurarum [ut dicit] Hostiensis, *Summa super titulis Decretalium*, de usuris, s. An aliquo, sub finem.

13. Quoniam eius arbitrio sunt determinanda, quae iure reliquuntur confusa lex 1, ff. De iure deliberandi [Dig. 28.8.1].

14. Ps. 36[:16]: Melius est modicum iusto super divitias peccatorum multas.

15. Matt. 16[:26]: Quid prodest homini, si universum mundum lucretur, animae vero suae detrimentum patiatur?

16. Ps. 36[:1]: Noli aemulari in malignantibus, et cetera.

11

Exchange by Buying, Bartering, or Innominate Contract

Summary

41. We declare that the same set of scales and measurements should be used to weigh and measure the justice of the exchange by buying as are used in the exchange by bartering, which is another innominate contract. On the one hand, buying and, on the other, bartering—which is an innominate contrac[2]—and the other innominate contracts, are different because buying is a contract specifically provided for by the law,[3] while the others are not. Consequently, in everything, contracts that are specifically provided for by the law for having a specific name[4] differ under the law from those that are not, and for this reason are called innominate.[5] There is no difference as far as our purpose is concerned, which is to see how it is possible to make a profit in a just way by buying, selling, or bartering money. Regarding this, it is the same to say it is a purchase as to say it is a barter or to say it is a contract where I give so that you give me, or I give or do so that you do, or so that you make someone else give me, or you do.

The contract by which one person gives to another in Medina 100 for 110 that the other person gives or has someone give to him in Flanders; or gives to him in Flanders 100 for having 120 given to him in Medina, becomes illicit for two reasons, or at least one:

1. the inequality of what is given and what is to be received; and
2. taking more or less for advancing or postponing, or for giving a long or short term to pay it back.

It is certain that these two things and each one of them make the bartering contract and any other contract specifically provided for by the law, such as the buying one, illicit, and also the opposite to the buying one, as with these others, for what was said above.[6]

42. The first conclusion is that there is no need to spend any time or to think any more about which opinion is truer: if the one that says that the next contract is a buying one, which is Cajetan's[7] opinion, and also Calderini's[8] and Laurencio's,[9] or a bartering one, as Soto[10] says, and before him Calderini and Laurencio,[11] or if it is an innominate contract: I give so that you give me, etc., which could perhaps be considered for what we said earlier[12] about exchange involving bills of exchange, and for other reasons that we could add.

The second conclusion is that in order to satisfy all opinions, we must use the word *commuting*,[13] which is common to all of the above operations and any other contract where one thing passes from one person to another.

The third conclusion is that said exchange (whatever it is called) is licit if it is carried out justly, and not if it is not. It is just when two things happen: First, that for the money commuted, the just value is given; and, second, that its value is not lowered for repaying it at a later date, as Cajetan[14] noted and, before him and best of all, Silvestre.[15] These reasons, even if they or others had not noted them, are proved by the two rules established above.[16]

43. The fourth conclusion is that the difficulty is in declaring how a profit can be made by commuting money by giving the just value for it. To which we respond that it may be done as with other merchandise, collecting it through exchange of its just value where or when it is worth less to exchange it where and when it is worth more. Saint Thomas[17] believes, and we have already said above,[18] that money (even insofar as it is money) may be commuted for money in order to gain a profit with it.

The fifth conclusion is that the solution of the aforementioned difficulty depends on knowing how and when a unit of money, which is equal to another according to the common price set by the law or custom at the time of coining it, is worth more or less for whatever reason than another unit of money. There is no way of knowing whether the exchange of a certain amount of money for another is just without knowing the value of both, because, as we explained earlier, in order for the exchange to be just, money should be bought for what it is worth.

This uncertainty regarding how and when a unit of money is worth more or less than another has eight causes:

1. for being of different metals,
2. for being of a different carat,
3. for being of a different weight and shape,
4. for the diversity of the land in which they circulate,
5. for the disapproval or doubt of disapproval regarding the increase or decrease of one of them,
6. for the diversity of time,
7. for the lack or need of it, and
8. for the absence of one and presence of the other.

44. Regarding the first cause, which is the difference in metal, sometimes a gold *ducat* is worth more to the one who has it than a silver or metal one because he can keep it better or take it far away; and the other way around, sometimes it is worth more to have a silver or another metal *ducat* than a gold one for the lack of small coinage to spend.[19]

Regarding the second cause, which is when the two coins are not the same carat metal, it happens that out of two *ducats*, which by law are appraised at the same value as the *ducats* from Castile, Portugal, Ungria, and Florence, one may be worth more than another, even if they are both in the same land.

Regarding the third, when they are a different weight and shape, sometimes a *ducat* with the same impression as another is worth more if it has an extra gram and a good shape, while the other lacks another gram or is broken, chipped, or disfigured.

Regarding the fourth, when they are in different lands, the same coin is worth more in one land than in another, according to Calderini's words.[20] This is because the metal in one land is worth more than in the other, such as gold is worth more in Spain than in the Indies, and more in France than in Spain because the king or one land's custom sets it at a higher price than the king or the custom in the other. This was the case when I studied in Toulouse, France. The king in that land manifestly raised the prices of his French *ducats* and those of the Spanish *ducats*, and they say he has gone on to raise them even more, and almost everyone agrees on this.[21]

45. Regarding the fifth cause, when there is disapproval regarding the value's increase, decrease, or doubt about it, we have seen in past years that the *tarjas* worth 10 had a lower value for some time than the one they had previously. In other lands, where there are many who mint coins, many times some of them order that the coins of their fellow towns may not circulate in their town. Others lower their price, and just as when after they order that it does not circulate any more, so then it is commuted for much less than before, so when they try to disapprove or lower the value and there is doubt regarding this, if it is done, it is commuted for something less. Just as after it rises, it is worth more, so when it is dealt with and there is doubt, it starts being commuted for something more. As certainly as the price rises for raising the value, and as certainly as it falls because of lowering the value, so when there is doubt regarding one or the other, there is an uncertain[22] increase and decrease. Commuting money that is worth more or less according to these five reasons is exchanging by true transference (which we discussed earlier),[23] and so I refer the reader to that discussion.

46. The sixth cause is the diversity of time because of which the value of money may rise or fall. Sometimes 100 gold *ducats* are worth more and sometimes less. The same is true for 100 silver *ducats* or 100 metal *ducats* or 100 units in absolute terms, which are worth more or less than what they will be in one year's time. They would be worth more (because of what was said earlier),[24] for any of the many reasons that there may be for this. For example, if for taking it from the ground to buy food, go to war, or help friends who go to war there were now a lack of some or all of them and then in a year there were an abundance for having sold the fruits and other merchandise from the ground or because the king has sufficiently paid his soldiers and servants, or for other similar causes. They would be worth less if there were now an abundance and, in one year's time, there were a scarcity, just as a measure of wheat is not worth as much in August when there is a great abundance of it, as in May when there is a scarcity of wheat, or less[25] of it.

47. But money is never said to be worth more or less for giving it before or after, or for a longer or shorter period of time, if any of the other eight reasons that make it increase or decrease is not attached to the time factor, according to almost everyone's opinion.[26]

The conclusion is that, in the first place, all the exchangers, merchants, and any others are wrong if they believe it is licit for them to take more than what they lent for having others keep their money for a longer period of time, without making use of it, and taking advantage of it. Thus, the exchangers make a mistake when they measure and count the time until the next fair, or until the payment day, when they are to be paid, in order to take more or less for the exchange.

48. In the second place, the person who lends 100 pieces of gold to another—and then the price of the pieces increases—may licitly ask for the greater value they have when he collects than when he lends them. He does not take a profit for the time lapse but for the increase of value—set by the king or by custom as time goes by—of what was owed to him. This is a conclusion that in many parts is taken from Bartolus,[27] who is widely accepted.[28] There is no doubt regarding this, if he intended to keep the money until then, as this chapter proves,[29] as do Juan Calderini and, in other parts, Gaspar Calderini[30] and Laurencio Rodulfo[31] and Silvestre,[32] whom Soto[33] reprimands, without quoting anyone for it, although Francisco Curcio Sr.[34] and others make reference to have held this opinion before him. Silvestre, however, does not deserve a reprimand because he refers to the person who lends the *ducats* that he was going to keep and because Soto's comparison (to our way of thinking) does not resolve the issue. Just as the person who lends a measure of wheat of 12 *celemines*[35] should not be repaid later a whole measure of 13 (even if it is ordered that the measure hold that amount),[36] so the person who lends a *ducat* worth 11 *reales* should not receive a *ducat* worth 12 if it is ordered that it is worth this amount before.

49. We believe this comparison is not irrefutable, because when the measure of wheat of 12 *celemines* is increased to 13, it changes its form and substance and stops being the same measure that it was before. Instead, when the *ducat* increases from 11 *reales* to 12 by order of the prince, it neither changes its substance or form nor stops being the same *ducat* it was at the beginning. What changes in it is something extrinsic and accidental, and does not belong to its essence, as Bartolus[37] holds, who is widely accepted.[38]

Because wheat does not stop being the same wheat as it was before, even if its appraisal grows or decreases, the person who borrows a measure of wheat has to give back another measure as good in its essence, even if it is worth more or less as far as price goes, which is something extrinsic to it. The metaphysical argument saying that price corresponds to the essence of the *ducat*, as *ducat* and coin, can be responded to with Bartolus's words, which are widely accepted. Even as coin, its essence is based more on its natural being than on its artificial one, as we have already stated.

We also say that such a lender may take that additional amount even if he had not intended on keeping the money, provided that he arranged that he would get back as many pieces and as various as the ones he had lent, whether they were worth more, less, or the same—at least if he did not have a greater certainty that its price would increase than that it would decrease, according to this chapter. This was like an adventure, a wager on what could happen, as everything is permissible.[39]

50. We go on to say that according to Bartolus's[40] common and widely accepted opinion,[41] the person who lends 100 gold *ducats* must receive them in the same quality of gold, without discounting anything from the price, even if the value increases and he had neither intended on keeping them nor expressly plans that they should be given back in such and so many pieces as he has given, whether they increase or decrease. The person who lends something should receive something of equal substance as what was lent, as good as it is (as far as the intrinsic goodness of it).[42] The intrinsic goodness of money does not issue from the price the republic sets on it but from the quality and goodness of the substance of which it is made, according to Bartolus's[43] true and accepted opinion.

Even if this accepted opinion could easily be held in all cases, we think it should be applied only in three of them:

1. when the person who lent them was going to put them away until the price went up;
2. when he expressly ordered that such and so many pieces as the ones he gave should be returned, whether

they increased or decreased the value, assuming the danger of losing, as well as the hope of winning; and

3. when the money's value increased so quickly, that even the person who borrowed it had not spent them, and was able to spend them and take advantage of them at the increased price.

Apart from these three cases, it is sufficient to pay the lender in the same pieces or other similar ones, or in the same metal as the ones he borrowed, and as many as there were at the time of the loan, giving the value they have at the time of the repayment. We hold these truths partly because of what Bartolus and the common[44] opinion hold, partly because of what Molinaeus says, and partly because of the great justice that[45] Baldo[46] wrote about, who declares it rightly.[47] We are not allowed to say any more (and, indeed, not even as much as we have already said) because of the brevity that we desire.

Notes

1. Ed. note: *hanega* = *fanega*: a capacity measurement for dry fruits, variable according to Spanish regions.

2. Lex Iuris gentium, cum glossa, ff. de pactis [Dig. 2.14.7]; lex Ex placito, C. De rerum permutatione cum glossa [Cod. 4.64.3].

3. Dicta lex Iuris gentium, in principio [Dig. 2.14.7]; lex Naturalis, s. Et siquidem, ff. De praescriptis verbis [Dig. 19.5.5.1].

4. Lex 1 et tribus sequentibus, ff. de praescriptis verbis [Dig. 19.5.1–4].

5. Quae sunt multa iuxta notata per Bartholum in dicta lege Naturalis, s. sed si facio [Dig. 19.5.5.4], no. 6, et per omnes in principio dictae legis Iuris gentium [Dig. 1.1.1–5], et glossam et alios in dicta lege Ex placito [Cod. 4.64.3].

6. See sections 14 and 24.

7. Cajetan, *De cambiis*, cap. 6 and 7.

8. Giovanni Calderini and Gaspar Calderini, *Consilia domini Iohannis Calderini et domini Gasparis eius filii redacta*, con. 11 [De usuris Rubrica].

9. Laurencio de Rodulfo, *Tractatus de usuris*, 3 parte, quaest. 1, c. Consuluit [*Dec. Greg.*, 5.19.10].

10. Soto, *De iustitia et iure*, lib. 7, quaest. 5, art. E. Cf. lib. 6, quaest. 12, art. 2 [fol. 594].

11. Laurencio de Rodulfo, *Tractatus de usuris*, 3 parte, quaest. 1, c. Consuluit [*Dec. Greg.*, 5.19.10].

12. See sections 21 and 22.

13. Ed. note: *comutar*: commuting in the sense of trading.

14. Cajetan, *De cambiis*, cap. 7.

15. Silvestre, *Sylvestrina suma, qua summa summarum merito nuncupatur*, verb. *usura* 4, quaest. 9.

16. See sections 14 and 24.

17. Thomas, *De regimine principum*, lib. 2, cap. 14, quem Antonius, Cajetan et omnes fere Theologi sequuntur; idem tenet Calderini, *Consilia*, con. 11, De usuris [Rubrica], et Laurencio de Rodulfo, *Tractatus de usuris*, in c. Consuluit [*Dec. Greg.*, 5.19.10], quaest. 1, parte 3, de usuris.

18. See sections 12 and 32.

19. Quod docet experientia rerum magistra: c. Quam sit, de electione [*Liber Sextus*, 1.6.6].

20. *Consilia*, con. 11, De usuris [Rubrica], quem sequitur Ioannes ab Annania in praesenti [De usuris Rubrica: *Dec. Greg.*, 5.19.19], no. 46 et sequentibus.

21. Conveniunt enim Antoninus, Silvestre, Cajetan, Medina et Soto, *De iustitia et iure*, lib. 6, quaest. 12, art. 2, fol. 594, et Laurencio de Rodulfo, *Tractatus de usuris*, quaest. 1, 3 partis c. Consuluit [*Dec. Greg.*, 5.19.10] de usuris [Rubrica], et Ioannes Annanias hic [De usuris Rubrica: *Dec. Greg.*, 5.19.19], no. 52.

22. Argumentum: lex si iactum retis, ff. De actionibus empti [Dig. 19.1.12], et capite praesenti cum ei annotatis.

23. See section 31.

24. See section 43.

25. C. In civitate, supra eodem [*Dec. Greg.*, 5.19.6] et in hoc capite [*Dec. Greg.*, 5.19.19].

26. Saint Thomas, *Summa theologicae*, II-II, quaest. 78, art. 1, 2, ad 7, et probatur in c. Ad nostram, de emptione [*Dec. Greg.*, 3.17.5].

27. In lege Cum quid, ff. de rebus creditis [Dig. 12.1.3], n. 7, et lege cum aurum, ff. de auro et argento [Dig. 34.2.19], et lege Paulus, ss. De solutionibus [Dig. 46.4.101], no. 6 et 10.

28. Per Baldum, Alexandrum, et Iasonem, et fere omnes alios in dicta lege Cum quid [Dig. 12.1.3].

29. S. ultimum, de usuris [*Dec. Greg.*, 5.19.19].

30. *Consilia*, con. 11, De usuris Rubrica.

31. In c. Consuluit, eodem titulo, 3 parte, quaest. 1 [*Dec. Greg.*, 5.19.10].

32. Silvestre, *Suma*, verb. *usura* 1, quaest. 14.

33. Soto, *De iustitia et iure*, lib. 6, quaest. 1, art. 1 [fol. 514]. Cf. lib. 7, quaest. 5, art. 1 [lib. 6, quaest. 12, art. 1, fol. 592].

34. In dicta lege Cum quid [Dig. 12.1.4] in tractatu monetae, col. 3, fol. 168.

35. Ed. note: *celemin*: a measure for dry goods that is equivalent to approximately 4.625 liters in Castile.

36. C. Cum canonicus, ubi glossa [*Dec. Greg.*, 3.39.6], et notatur in c. Olim. [*Dec. Greg.*, 3.39.30], et in c. Ex parte, de censibus [*Dec. Greg.*, 3.39.18].

37. In lege Quod te, no. 7, ff. de rebus creditis [Dig. 12.1.5].

38. Ait etiam Molinaeus [Charles du Moulin] id servatum his tribus saeculis, *Tractatus commerciorum et usurarum, redituumque pecunia constitutorum, and monetarum*, no. 696.

39. Argumentum: lex Si iactum retis, ff. De actionibus empti [Dig. 19.1.12], et huius c [Cod. 4.33], et lex Periculi, ff. De nautico foenore [Dig. 22.2.5]. Et quae tradit Molinaeus [Charles du Moulin], *Tractatus commerciorum*, n. 718 et sequentibus.

40. In lege Cum quid, ff. de rebus creditis, no. 7 [Dig. 12.1.5], et lege 1 et Lege Cum Aurum, ff. de auro et argento [Dig. 34.2.19], et lege Paulus, ff. de solutionibus, no. 6 et 10 [Dig. 46.4.101].

41. Per Baldum, Alexandrum, Iasonem et fere omnes alios in dicta lege Cum quid [Dig. 12.1.3], Ioannem Calderinum in c. Si, de usuris [Cod. 4.32.1], et Laurentium Rodulfum in c. Consuluit [*Dec. Greg.*, 5.19.10] 3 parte, quaest. 1, et Panormitanum cum communi in c. Quanto, de iure iurando [*Dec. Greg.*, 2.24.18].

42. In dicta lege Cum quid [Dig. 12.1.3], et lege Virum, ff. de rebus creditis [Dig. 12.1.22].

43. In lege Quod te, no. 7, ff. de rebus creditis [Dig. 12.1.5], quod Molinaeus [Charles du Moulin] ait servatum his tribus saeculis, *Tractatus commerciorum*, no. 696.

44. In dicta lege Cum quid [Dig. 12.1.3].

45. Baldus de Ubaldis, *De commerciis*, quaest. 90, 92a, no. 694.

46. In authentico, Ad haec, quaest. 17, De usuris.

47. Baldus de Ubaldis, *De commerciis*, no. 707.

12

The Value of Money

Summary

51. The next thing that we say regards the seventh motive of why money increases or decreases its value. That happens when there is great lack or need (or an abundance of it). It is worth more where and when there is a great lack of it than where there is a great abundance, as declare Calderini,[3] Laurencio Rodulfo,[4] and Silvestre,[5] with whom Cajetan[6] and Soto[7] agree.

From them follow several opinions:

First, this is what most of the good and evil men of Christendom think, and thus it seems to be the voice of God and nature.[8]

Second, and very obviously, all merchandise becomes more expensive when there is a great need and small quantity of it.[9] Money, inasmuch as it is a thing that may be sold, bartered, or commuted by means of another contract, is merchandise for the reasons we gave above[10] and may also become more expensive when there is a great need of it and yet not enough to satisfy this need.

Third, all other things being equal, in those countries where there is a great lack of money, less money is given for marketable goods, and even for the hands and work of men, than where there is an abundance of it. This we can see from experience in France where there is less money than in Spain. Bread, wine, wool, hands, and work cost less. Even in Spain, when there was less money, much less was given for saleable goods, and the hands and work of men, than later when the discoveries of the Indies covered it in silver and gold. The cause for this is that money is worth more where and when there is a lack of it than where and when there is an abundance. That which some say, that the lack of money reduces the price of everything, is born of the fact that its more than sufficient increase makes everything appear much lower, just as a small man next to a very tall man appears smaller than if he were next to his equal.

52. Fourth, the lack of gold coins may surely increase their value, so that more silver coins, or coins of another metal, have to be offered for the gold coins,[11] as we see now that because of the lack of gold coins, some give 22 and even 23 and 25 *reales* for a *doubloon*, which by the kingdom's price and law is not worth more than 22.

We have even seen in Portugal 11½ silver *ducats*, and even 12, offered for 10 *ducats* of another kind. The shortage of silver coins may increase their value so that more gold coins or metal coins have to be given than before for the silver ones. Even the shortage of small copper coins or other cheap metals may have their value increase so that more gold or silver has to be given than before for them. This we have seen in Portugal where, when there was an abundance of *cetis*, 106 *maravedis* in *cetis* were given for 1 *teston*,[12] which is not worth more than 100. Then, when there was a shortage of *cetis*, we gave 1 *teston* for 94 in *cetis*. So, it seems that when money in general is scarce, the price of the different coins in general increases.[13]

Fifth, there is a law[14] that establishes this. After saying that the reason why there is arbitrary action in asking in one place for something that must be paid somewhere else is because something is worth more in one place than in another (mainly if it is bread, wine, or oil), the law goes on to say the following about money: "Although the value of money also seems to be one and the same everywhere, nevertheless in some places it is more abundant and lighter usuries are found, and in other places it is more scarce and more severe usuries are found."[15]

53. There are many arguments against this opinion, and, because of these, we used to think it was unreasonable. The first objection against it is that no matter how much or how scarce money is, a *ducat* is never worth more or less than 11 *reales* and 1 *maravedi* here or in Rome, Flanders, or León. It is never worth more or less than what the pope, the king, or custom has appraised it for, and it will not be taken for a higher value from the person who sells you something. Also, it is objected that in holding the above opinion, we are forced to say what some people[16] believe, namely, that there are two types of *ducats* and *escudos*: The first is the one used by merchants for their exchanges, which rises or falls according to the abundance or shortage of money. Consequently, depending on the situation, either many or few want to give or take in exchange. The second type are those *ducats* and *escudos* intended to be spent by the people and even by the merchants themselves in those expenses that are not exchanges, which always have a fixed price. This seems a tenuous belief because the Roman, ecclesiastical, or secular jurisdiction never considered it.[17] Since merchants do not have the power to increase or decrease public money,[18] it sounds like something fleeting—a trap, a veil, and cover of usuries to feign *ducats* or *escudos*—to give them an imagined value so that no one who sells bread, wine, meat, fish, cloth, or any other thing will take them except by way of exchange to pay them back in another fair or place. There does not seem to be a solid reason why, except for a lack of money in general, that a greater quantity of *ducats* and *escudos* are imagined only for exchanging them without there being another use for spending them. Thus, in exchanging them, a cloud is formed in order to cover the loan that is carried out with usury under it. Also against the earlier opinion is the fact that money considered as money seems to be the price of all other merchandise[19] but is not itself merchandise, and its price is not appraised[20] in each kingdom, and thus, may not increase more than wheat when it is appraised by the republic.

54. Regardless of these objections and Doctor Medina's[21] contrary opinion (which, at one time, we thought was better), we hold the first opinion because of the new reasons and considerations in favor of it. To the first objection, which seems insoluble, we may respond that even if or when there is a shortage of money in general, a *ducat* should not be worth more *reales* than when there is an abundance of money, neither should the *real* be worth more *quartos*, nor the *quartos*[22] more *maravedis*. All money is worth more because more saleable goods may be found for a fraction of what they were worth before, all else being equal. This is not to say that the increase in the price of money is due to the decrease in the other thing's prices, because it is this decrease that follows the increase in the price of money, as we have considered in the third argument above.

To the second objection, which seems insoluble, we may respond by denying that it is necessary in order to defend this opinion to introduce imagined and chimerical *ducats* and *escudos*, which as Plato's ideas, find themselves in specie and genre, and not individually, as the arguments rightly conclude. It is confirmed effectively with the consideration that whoever says this must confess that almost as many imaginary *ducats* must be fabricated as places money is given and taken for in the fair. There is almost a different price for each place: one for Flanders, another for Rome, another for León, another for Lisbon, another for Valencia, another for Zaragoza, and so forth. A comical thing adding to this consideration is that it seems it has not been said enough that the *ducat* or *escudo* are not worth as much in the fair if they are not worth as much for such and such a place. Even those who say this mean that the *ducat* is given for such and such a place for the barter or price that is given for it in one place.

55. To the third objection, we answer by denying that money considered as money should always be considered as the price of things, because, even considered as money, it may be commuted by buying, bartering, or with a contract specifically provided for by the law or an innominate contract, as was said above.[23] Although it is true that its main and principal use and end for which it was created was as price and measure of saleable goods,[24] its secondary and less principal use and end, which is that of making a profit with it by dealing money for money, is not to be price but merchandise, just as the principal use and end of shoes is to put them on and wear them, but the secondary one is to make a profit by dealing with them through buying and selling them. As far as the value is concerned, we will respond to it below.[25]

56. The following conclusions are derived from the above:

First, that the gold coin, because of the specific shortage of it, may be worth more than it would be worth if there were an abundance of it; and the silver coin, because of the specific shortage of it, as well as the metal one, for its shortage, and all coins in general for their general shortage.

Second, there is no need to feign merchants' imaginary *ducats* or *escudos* that are different from those the people use. Without them, it is still possible to clearly set a price for a *ducat* or *escudo* for one party and for the other. Moreover, it is more advisable not to feign them so that those who lend and give money unjustly do not have the chance to be repaid at the value they decide to fix, as Doctor Soto[26] tacitly expressed.

Third, the exchange that many carry out is usury, who according to them give to some people *ducats* or *escudos* from one fair to the next to be paid at the price that they are worth when they are given, or at the price that the merchants' ones are worth in the market when they are to be paid, because there are no such *ducats* or *escudos* in the world, and because, if they existed, they would be as diverse in value as the cities between which they are exchanged. For between some cities, they are exchanged for an equal value, such as many times happens from Medina to Lisbon. For others, at 10 or 20 *maravedis*; for others at 30; and for others at 40 and 50. They even give them sometimes at the price they get for exchanging them in the city where they are worth the most. Moreover, the reason that justifies the commutation of a sum of money that has to be given in a far away city does not justify the commutation of a similar amount that has to be given in the same city, for the reason we will state below.[27] Although it should be confessed that whoever finds someone who takes his money for a true exchange and does not gain a profit with him because of giving it to his neighbor or another close person who greatly needs it, may in such manner earn with it what he is prevented from earning with the other person, for the reason we gave above.[28]

57. Fourth, the value of money may not only increase or decrease inasmuch as it is a piece of metal, but even inasmuch as it is money and price of the rest of things. The majority of the eight motives because of which money increases or decreases are motives that pertain to money as money and price of saleable goods and conclude that inasmuch as it is money and price, it is worth more in one land than in another, and even in one land more at one time than in another.

Fifth, there is a need to explain that compelling argument against this that is based on the price, whose solution above we restate here. The argument is that money is appraised, and things are appraised, as wheat is usually, that do not increase due to a lack of it. Some of the aforementioned[29] respond that even it is appraised inasmuch as it is price. It is not appraised inasmuch as it is merchandise. This is not satisfactory, however. For the reasons stated above, it is evident that even inasmuch as it is money and price, it may increase or decrease. Silvestre[30] declares that money is appraised inasmuch as it is price of other saleable goods but not inasmuch as it is price of money itself. He does not explain why there is such difference. Others[31] believe that money should never be sold, and thus some would say that there is not a higher price in its commutation. On the one hand, this goes against the common practice,[32] which refers to buying and selling money. On the other hand, it is not convenient to those who hold this position at all. If they confess that there is barter and that you cannot barter but for what something is worth, that its value increases for its greater worth due to its great lack, and that more should be given the more it is worth,[33] they have to forcefully confess that its value increases regardless of its price, and thus have the same need of explaining the argument based on its price as do those who say you can buy it.

58. Thus, we answer again, conceding that money is appraised for one end and not for another. It is appraised in order to compel the person who sells something or to whom something is owed to take the money for said price so that he cannot be compelled to take it for more. It is neither appraised in order that the person who has it cannot take less for it if he so desires, nor in order that he cannot take more if he gains an advantage by this. This solution cannot reassure the consciences of those who commute it for a higher price for the shortage of it without there being an advantage in keeping it, even if the person with whom one is commuting it obtains an advantage in getting paid. The seller cannot sell the thing more expensively for the personal gain that this may bring to the buyer, although he may sell it more expensively for the benefit he loses in selling it, according to what Saint Thomas[34] and Scotus[35] said. We see every day the dealers who frequently obtain a benefit from saving their money when there is great lack of it (even if it means only buying some things at a cheaper price). We see even those who are not dealers commute at present the *doubloons* for 24 and 25 *reales*, when they are actually appraised at 22, for the great lack of them. Though it might be said that the *doubloons* are worth more for the intrinsic value of their gold, which is much higher than that of the *coronas*,[36] we would not be able to say the same of the rest of the other coins, though they increase or decrease every day, as Bartolus[37] and Panormitanus[38] say, whom no one contradicts. Therefore, it seems safer to respond that money is appraised so that, all else being equal, it is not worth more in one place, but not such that it cannot be worth more when it changes so much that there is great lack and need of that appraised money,[39] which seems so to wise and good men, at least in order to commute it for other money, as Silvestre says.

59. Sixth, it is not unusual that money (even inasmuch as it is money) is worth more in one fair than in another and more in one part of the same fair than in another part. It may be that in one part it is worth less because few people want to take it for true exchange, and many want to give it; and in another part it may be worth more because of there being many who want to take it for true exchange and few who want to give it. The price of money increases for great need or lack of it.[40] We say "true exchange" because we believe that the price of money should not be increased when there are a great many people who want to take it for feigned and illicit exchanges, as deception and fraud should not bring profit to the one who commits them.[41] No merchandise becomes more expensive when there are many who want to steal it or illicitly usurp it, although it does become more expensive when there are many who want to justly buy it or barter it.[42] As Doctor Soto[43] stated wisely, money should not be more expensive at the fair for a lack of it or for an absence of people who want to give it when this lack is born of the illicit conspiracy of those who have to give it and of the exchangers who openly or covertly decide not to give it until it is more expensive.[44] Nor should it be more expensive because at the beginning of the fair, when everything is cheaper for everybody, they took most of it, and then, as they are in possession of most of it, do not want to give it except as they please. In this case, those who are not guilty may give it in good conscience according to its lack, but not those who are guilty[45]—something that happens more often than it should.

60. Seventh, it would be even less surprising if the *ducat* were worth more in Portugal than in Castile, although there is doubt if it is. First, because the person who in Portugal owes 400 *reales* may pay them with a *ducat* worth 11 *reales*, and the person who owes and to whom is owed 400 *maravedis* here cannot pay them here or there with 1 *ducat*. This means that the *maravedis* from here are worth more than the *reales* from there, but the *ducat* is worth the same here as there and there as here. In His Majesty's provision to moderate exchanges, whose content we referred to earlier,[46] it is established that 370 *maravedis* from here are worth 400 *reales* over there.

We think the opposite is truer, that is, that the *ducat* from here and from there is worth more there than here; also that the *real* from here is worth more there than here because the *ducat* is worth 400 *reales* from there and the *real* 36, and here the *ducat* is worth only 375 *maravedis* and the *real* 34. That the *reales* from there and *maravedis* from here are equal is inferred from the fact that as a *real* is worth in Portugal 6 *cetis*, so the *maravedi* (now in use) is worth 6 *cornados*, which apparently are equal to the *cetis*, as the holy Archbishop Don Diego de Leyva y Covarrubias seems to efficiently prove.[47] Today, in the kingdom of Galicia (where there are *cetis* as in Portugal) 6 *cetis* are worth 1 *maravedi*. In Portugal, too, they are worth 1 *real*. Also, what those who object to this view allege is not pertinent.[48] We deny that the person who owes in Portugal 400 *reales* does just payment here with 1 *ducat* if he is not satisfied with it. We even deny that there is just payment when the one to whom you owe there 11 *reales* receives another 11 that you pay him here. We also deny that the person who owes here 400 *maravedis* does just payment there with 400 *reales*.

Also, it is possible to respond to the provision to moderate exchanges that such words were included there by accident.[49] If you reply that its determination[50] is based on it, we will say that it is based on someone else's acts and that the opposite[51] may be proved. We believe that even if this is accepted in these kingdoms for their benefit, it will be not be accepted in the foreign ones, even if those kingdoms belong to His Majesty, because it will harm them.

61. Eighth, it is extremely important that whoever lends in Portugal 100 *ducats* is able to take for them in Medina more than 100 for the only reason that they are worth more there than here.[52]

Ninth, whoever lends 100 *ducats* in Medina should not receive 100 in Lisbon because they are worth more there than here,[53] and whoever lends may not take more than what he lent.[54]

Tenth, what has been said about Medina and Lisbon in these two last conclusions should also be said of any other two cities where the same currency is worth more in one of them than in the other. Thus, the person who lends 100 *ducats* in Flanders, Rome, or León (where the *ducats* are worth more than in Castile) should be paid more than 100 in Castile. So also the other way around: the person who lends 100 in Castile should not get paid 100 in Rome, concerning which Doctor Soto notably agrees.[55] Just as it would be usury to lend you a load[56] of wheat in Salamanca (where it is worth 2 *ducats*) so that you pay it to me in Galizia where it is worth 4, so it would be usury to lend you here a *ducat* worth 375 *maravedis* so that you pay it back to me somewhere else where it is worth 400. Just as it is injustice (although it is not usury, but injustice) that for a load of wheat that I lent to you in Galizia where it was worth 4 *ducats* you pay me with another one here in Salamanca where it is not worth more than 2, so it is injustice that for 100 *ducats* that you lent me in Rome or Lisbon where they are worth 400 I give you but 100 in Medina where they are not worth more than 375.

Eleventh, he who lends a certain quantity of wheat, wine, and oil where it is worth more should get back a greater amount if he is paid where they are worth less, depending on how much more it is worth where he lends than where he is being paid.[57] He who lends where something is worth less, should receive a smaller quantity if he is paid where it is worth more, depending on how much more it is worth where he is getting paid than where he lends. Thus, he who lends *ducats* where they are worth more, should receive as much more if he is paid where they are worth less as the greater value of those *ducats* amounts to. So, too, the other way around: he who lends *ducats* where they are worth less, should receive as much less if he is paid where they are worth more as that greater value amounts to.

Twelfth, because of this, it may seem to some that there is no doubt in Doctor Soto's conclusion[58] that he who gives for exchange in Spain a *ducat*, which is only worth 11 *reales*, so that he gets paid back in Rome another worth 12 or 13 *carlines*[59]—which are equal to our *reales*, or are worth more than 11—commits usury because he wants to take more than what he gives and gain an extra amount. Neither this conclusion, however, nor the ones that follow from it, can be inferred from our deductions. Nor do we believe they are indisputable. They do not follow from the above because the three deductions refer to the one who lends money and to the loan that in Latin is called *mutuum*, whose very nature is gratuitous. By virtue of it, nothing more than what was loaned should be taken, as we said in another commentary.[60] Soto's conclusion talks about the one who gives in an exchange that is not gratuitous in nature, and that is why it cannot be inferred from them; they each refer to different things.[61] This is not a true doctrine because everyday the opposite is done from Medina to Lisbon and Flanders and from there to Medina, the practice of which is licit whether by way of real purchase or by way of barter or other innominate contracts, as we go on to prove below.[62]

Notes

1. Ed. note: Syncopated form of *coronado*. Castilian vellum coin, thus called for showing the head of the crowned king. It was equivalent to 6 *cornados*, 1 *maravedi* in the fifteenth century.
2. Ed. note: *ceitil*: a copper coin minted by Alfonso V from Portugal (1438–1481), as Lord of Ceuta; *ceita* or *capta*: a copper coin belonging to Juan II of Portugal (1419–1490), equivalent to one-sixth of a *real*. This measure continued until D. Sebastián (1557–1578).
3. Giovanni Calderini and Gaspar Calderini, *Consilia domini Iohannis Calderini et domini Gasparis eius filii redacta*, con. 11 [De usuris Rubrica].
4. In. c. Consuluit [*Dec. Greg.*, 5.19.10], quaest. 1, 3 partis.
5. Verb. *usura* 4, quaest. 5 et 6, vers. pro notitia.
6. Cajetan, *De cambiis*, cap. 6 s. De temporis, 166.
7. Soto, *De iustitia et iure*, lib. 7, quaest. 5, art. 2 et 3; lib. 6, quaest. 12, art. 2ff.
8. Iuxta illud: vox populi, vox naturae, quae Deus est; iuxta glossam legis 1, ff. de iustitia et iure, verb. *natura* [Dig. 1.1.1].
9. C. Legimus, 93 dist. Ibi: omne rarum pretiorum facit, cap. Praesens [*Dec. Grat.*, 1.93.24.2]: omne quod rarum est, plus appetitur. Pulegium apud Indos pipera pretiosius est, cum ei annotatis.
10. See sections 12 and 20.
11. Laurencio de Rodulfo, *Tractatus de usuris*, quaest. 1, 3 parte [*Dec. Greg.*, 5.19.10]. Annanias, *Commentaria super prima et secunda parte libri V Decretalium*, no. 52 [*Dec. Greg.*, 5.19.19].
12. Ed. note: In Portuguese, *tostao*. Silver coins minted since the time of D. Manuel (1495–1521) that weighed 9.96 grams.
13. Quia regulariter, quod valet species in specie, id valet genus in genere, c. Quando, 24 dist. [*Dec. Grat.*, 1.24.5], ut habet glossa, et Imolensis in c. sic sacerdos, de officio iudicis ordinarii [*Dec. Greg.*, 1.31.2].

14. Lex 4, ff. de eo, quod certo loco dari opotet, a nemine in hoc citata [Dig. 13.4.3].

15. *Pecuniarum quoque, licet videatur una et eadem potestas ubique esse, tamen aliis locis facilius, et levioribus usuris inveniuntur, aliis, difficilius, et gravioribus usuris.* [Digest 13.4.3]

16. Silvestre, *Sylvestrina suma, qua summa summarum merito nuncupatur*, verb. *usura* 4, quaest. 6, cui concordat Cajetan, *De cambiis*, cap. 5, fol. 165 et Soto, *De iustitia et iure*, lib. 6, quaest. 12, art. 2 [fol. 594 s.].

17. Cuius modi novitates parum probantur, c. Cum consuetudinis, de consuetudine [*Dec. Greg.*, 1.4.9], et c. Quis nesciat, dist. 11 [*Dec. Grat.*, 1.12.2].

18. Iuxta mentem Innocentii, et communem in c. Quanto, de iureiurando [*Dec. Greg.*, 2.24.16], et Thomas, *De regimine principum*, lib. 2, c. 13; tradit Gabriel Biel, *Commentarii doctissimi in IV sententiarum libros*, dist. 15, quaest. 9; Molinaeus [Charles du Moulin], *Tractatus commerciorum et usurarum, redituumque pecunia constitutorum, and monetarum*, no. 193.

19. Lex Si tibi, ff. De fideiussoribus [Dig. 46.1.42], Aristotle 1 politicorum, 6 [Aristotle, *Politics*, trans. E. Barker (Oxford: Clarendon, 1948), 1.9 = Didot ed., 1:490], Saint Thomas, *De regimine principum*, lib. 2, cap. 13 et 14, et Laurencio de Rodulfo, *Tractatus de usuris*, in c. Consuluit [*Dec. Greg.*, 5.19.10] 2 parte, quaest. 26.

20. Iuxta mentem textus Innocentii, et aliorum in c. Quanto, de iureiurando [*Dec. Greg.*, 2.24.18].

21. Medina, *Codex de Restitutione et Contractibus*, fol. 150 [An pecunia vendi possit, fol. 157].

22. Ed. note: Copper coin, primitively made of vellum, from Castile, worth 4 *maravedis*, coined from the fifteenth to the nineteenth centuries.

23. See sections 11, 12, and 32.

24. Lex Si tibi, ff. De fideiussoribus [Dig. 46.1.42], et supra eodem no. 11 est dictum et habetur 1 politicorum [Aristotle, *Politics*, 1.9 = Didot ed., 1:490], et Thomas, *De regimine principum*, lib. 2, cap. 13 et 14.

25. See sections 57 and 58.

26. Soto, *De iustitia et iure*, lib. 5, quaest. 5, art. Cf. lib. 6, quaest. 12, art. 1 [fol. 595].

27. See section 65.

28. See section 26.

29. E quibus est Cajetan, *De cambiis*, cap. 6.

30. Silvestre, *Suma*, verb. *usura* 4, quaest. 3.

31. Soto, *De iustitia et iure*, lib. 7, quaest. 5, art. 2. Cf. lib. 6, quaest. 12, art. 2 [fol. 594].

32. Bartholus, in lege Paulus 1, ff. de solutionibus [Dig. 46.3.101], no. 7 et 10, et Panormitanus in c. Quanto, de iureiurando [*Dec. Greg.*, 2.24.18], no. 13; Thomas, *Summa theologicae*, II-II, quaest. 78, art. 2 ad 4; Calderini, *Consilia*, con. 11, De usuris [Rubrica].

33. Quae omnia praedictus Soto fatetur in dicto articulo 2, lib. 6, quaest. 12 [fol. 594].

34. Thomas, *Summa theologicae*, II-II, quaest. 77, art. 1, 3.

35. Scotus, *Quaestiones in quattuor libros sententiarum*, lib. 4, dist. 15, quaest. 2.

36. Ed. note: Gold *escudo* piece carved by Charles I in 1535 at a ratio of 68 for *marco* and a value of 350 *maravedis* and a weight of 22 carats.

37. In lege Paulus, ff. de solutionibus [Dig. 46.4.101].

38. In c. Quanto, no. 13, de iureiurando [*Dec. Greg.*, 2.24.18].

39. Argumentum: c. Ne quis, 22, quaest. 2 [*Dec. Grat.*, 2.22.2.14], et lex Cum quis, ff. De solutionibus [Dig. 46.3.38], et C. Quemadmodum, de iureiurando, cum glossis [*Dec. Greg.*, 2.24.25].

40. Cajetan, *De cambiis*, cap. 7, 166, et Soto, *De iustitia et iure*, lib. 7, quaest. 5, art. 3. Cf. lib. 6, quaest. 12, art. 3 [fol. 599].

41. C. Ex tenore, de rescriptis [*Dec. Greg.*, 1.3.16], c. Adversus, de immunitate ecclesiarum [*Dec. Greg.*, 3.49.7].

42. Late Cajetan, *Summa*, II-II, quaest. 77, art. 1.

43. Soto, *De iustitia et iure*, lib. 6, quaest. 12, art. 3 [fol. 599].

44. Argumentum: Lex 1, C. de monopoliis [Cod. 4.59.1].

45. Quia fraus et dolus nemini prodesse debent, c. Ex tenore, de rescriptis [*Dec. Greg.*, 1.3.16]; lex itaque fullo, ff. de furtis [Dig. 47.2.12].

46. See section 30.

47. Diego de Leyva y Covarrubias, *Variarum Resolutionum Liber Primus*, cap. 11, no. 4.

48. See section 72.

49. Et ita non probant c. Si Papa, de privilegiis lib. 6 [*Liber Sextus*, 5.7.10].

50. Et ita probant clementinae 1, de probationibus.

51. Iuxta glossam dictae clementinae 1.

52. Argumentum bonum in lege 3, s. Nunc de officio, ff. de eo, quod certo loco [Dig. 13.4.2.8], et melius in lege 4 eiusdem tituli.

53. Argumentarum praedictarum legum [Dig. 12.4.2, 4].

54. Azpilcueta, *Comentario Resolutorio de Usuras*, cap. 1, 14, quaest. 2 [*Dec. Grat.*, 2.14.3.1] cum his quae ibi late dicebamus, no. 7, 85.

55. Soto, *De iustitia et iure*, lib. 6, quaest. 5, art. 1. Cf. lib. 6, quaest. 10, art. 1 [fol. 592].

56. Ed. note: *carga*: a certain quantity of grain, which in some places has the capacity of 4 *fanegas*, and in others, 3.

57. Lex 3, s. Nunc de officio, ff. De eo quod certo loco [Dig. 13.4.2.8].

58. Soto, *De iustitia et iure*, lib. 7, quaest. 3, art. 1. Cf. lib. 6, quaest. 10, art. 1 [fol. 587].

59. Ed. note: A certain silver coin minted in the time of Emperor Charles V.

60. Azpilcueta, *Comentario Resolutorio de Usuras*, cap. 1, 14 quaest. 3 [*Dec. Grat.*, 2.14.3.1], no. 3 per illum textum, 7, et c. Consuluit, eodem titulo [*Dec. Greg.*, 5.19.10] et alia multa.

61. Nam a separatis non fit illatio: lex Papiniamus, ff. de minoribus [Dig. 4.4.20], c. Sententia, de sentential excommunicationis, lib. 6 [*Liber Sextus*, 5.2.16].

62. See section 74.

13

Money That Is Present and Money That Is Absent

Summary

62. As for the eighth motive[1] explaining why the value of money increases or decreases, which is that of its absence, Silvestre[2] believes more absolutely than anyone else that only its absence lowers its price in the place where it is absent. Even if some may believe something else, Cajetan[3] agrees with us, and before all of them Calderini[4] and Laurencio Rodulfo,[5] and we think it juridical.

On the one hand, all merchandise that is absent and is purchased to bring to the place where one is, considered in its entirety, requires by its very nature expenses and work, estimated in monetary terms,[6] to retrieve and bring it. Despite the possibility that the merchant may have relatives, friends, or agents to retrieve it in the place where it is absent, without any expense or work on his part, all these people end up getting paid in one way or another, and for this the merchant is indebted to do the same for them, at least under the obligation to make compensation.[7] A job does not stop having a price even if someone does it gratuitously.[8] By justice one cannot take away what has been promised to someone for going from here to Rome by saying that on the way he found someone to pay for his expenses and even to give him money to accompany him.

On the other hand, no one will say that a mule that is in Seville is not worth less for the person who is here than another mule that is present of the same quality and price, even if by some accidental case or because of his skill he may bring it here without expenses or it may cost more over there than here. It is true that if no skill, custom, or provision of merchants were involved in this, money from Flanders would be worth much less here than what it is worth, and it is unfair for the merchants' activity to hurt anyone.[9]

63. Also, Doctor Medina[10] is not an impediment when he says that the money's absence from the place is not enough on its own to make it worth less. The absence together with the dangers that occur and the expenses incurred to recover the absent money are sufficient cause to make it worth less than the money that is present. Because our words follow his, the expenses and work involved are as joined to its absence as we state and prove, even if some of these expenses and work accidentally detach themselves from the absence.

Also, it is not an impediment either that Doctor Soto[11] holds that neither the absence on its own (as Medina says) makes it worth less, nor the dangers and expenses, because such dangers and expenses are not present today among merchants. From the logic of his saying, we arrive at our conclusion. He confesses *a contrario sensu* that if those dangers and expenses existed, money would be worth more, and with our first reasoning we prove that they do in fact exist, given the nature of the business, and even considering the expenses for where they take it of the agents and representatives whom the merchant has over there.

There is no impediment in his argument that if this were true, the money from Flanders in Medina would be worth less than the money from Medina itself, which is false, because according to what he says a *ducat* from Flanders is worth more in Medina for which more than 400 *maravedis* are given in Medina, than a *ducat* from Medina itself obtained for 375. We say, thus, that this is no impediment because we deny what is inferred. We do not mean to say that all absent money is always worth less than the present one, but that it is worth less when all else is equal, namely, when the money that is present is worth the same where it happens to be as the money that is absent where it happens to be, and not any other way.

A load of wheat in Toro is worth less to the one who is here than another load that is present, if all else is equal. This is true if both are the same quality, and the one over there is equal in worth to the one that is here, but it is not true if the load of wheat in Toro is worth 4 *ducats* over there and here no more than 2 and if he could have it brought securely for 1. Then it would be worth more, but a little less than the 4 *ducats*, for being absent. Thus, if the *ducat* from Flanders were not worth more in Flanders than the one from Medina in Medina, the *ducat* from Flanders would be worth less in Medina than another *ducat* from this city. It is worth so much more in Flanders than in Medina that even if for its absence its price might be diminished, it will not be so diminished that it still is not worth more than the one from Medina.

64. From which follows:

First, Calderini[12] did well in advising that a good purchase was that of one who bought 106 *ducats* from Alexandria from another in Genoa for 100 *ducats*, because the 100 present *ducats* from Genoa were worth more for the person who was here than 100 that were absent, in Alexandria.

Second, if the exchanges from one part of the kingdom to another in the same kingdom were not, as they say they are, forbidden, one would be able to buy from a Sevillian in Burgos, Medina, or here with 100 *ducats* more than 100 *ducats* that had to be given in Seville. The *ducat* is worth as much here as there, and no more, and the absence lowers the price of money that is over there.

Third, the farther away the money, the lower its price, and the more dangers and expenses to recover it and pay for its transportation. Thus, in Salamanca the money that is in Medina will cost more than the one in Burgos; and the money in Burgos will cost more than the one in Seville; and the money in Seville will cost more than the one in Alexandria, Rome, Flanders, or León. The farther away it is, the more difficult it is to collect and the greater the cost of transporting it essentially, and the closer it is, the easier and lesser it is. We said "essentially" because it may happen accidentally that something that is farther away may be easier to collect, but it is important to take notice more of the essence[13] than of the accident of the business.

65. Fourth, the absence of money that is in Flanders makes it worth less in Medina to the one who is there and buys it there than it would be worth in Flanders to the person who is there and buys it there. It is frequently not worth so much less that it is not worth more in Medina than the *ducat* from Medina. Even if its absence (all else being equal) makes that which is absent worth less than that which is present, the difference is not so significant, since the *ducat* is worth more there than in Medina.

Fifth, the reason why the *ducats* from Flanders are frequently worth more in Medina than those same in Medina is that the *ducats* are worth so much more there than here. Even if the absence takes something away from its price, it does not take away so much that it is not always worth much more.

Sixth, the reason why the exchange is cheaper from here to Flanders than from Flanders to here is that 100 *ducats* from Medina cost less in Flanders than 100 from Flanders in Medina. The reason for this is that the price of 100 *ducats* from Medina proposed to be sold in Flanders diminishes for two reasons: one, because of their absence, and two, because the *ducat* is worth less in Medina than in Flanders, and the price of the *ducats* from Flanders proposed to be sold in Medina do not diminish except for one reason: their absence, which even if it makes them worth somewhat less is not so much given that they are worth more over there than here.

66. Seventh is the reason why many times there is a par exchange from Medina to Lisbon, that is, as many *ducats* are exchanged for as many others: 100 in Medina for another 100 given in Lisbon and no more or less. The reason for this is that the price of money from Lisbon proposed to be sold in Medina is lower than in Lisbon for being absent and outside of the kingdom. The reason why the exchange to Flanders is never, or very few times, equal (even if it is absent and outside of the kingdom) is that it is worth more in Flanders than in Lisbon, and even if the absence and being outside of the kingdom are sufficient to make the money from Lisbon equal to that of Medina in Medina, not even the absence or being outside of the kingdom are sufficient to make the price of the money from Medina equal to that of Flanders.

67. Eighth, the above said does not apply to the exchange carried out in such a way that in one and the same place the money is given from one person to another and from the other to the first, whether the place where the agreement is to occur is determined for this or another that is farther away or nearer to it. So it only applies when it is agreed in such a way that the money belonging to one is given in one place to another, and in another place the money belonging to another is given to the other, as Cajetan[14] clearly stated. This had already been noted abundantly with no additional help because the reason for expenses, work, and dangers on which the diminishment of the value of absent money is based cannot be applied when in one and the same place the delivery of both parts is carried out, but in order to pay (when there are many places involved) so much for the money as is paid in the exchange for small coinage, to which we referred above.[15]

Notes

1. Ed. note: See the list of eight causes in section 43.
2. Silvestre, *Sylvestrina suma, qua summa summarum merito nuncupatur*, verb. *usura* 4, quaest. 4.
3. Cajetan, *De cambiis*, cap. 7.
4. Giovanni Calderini and Gaspar Calderini, *Consilia domini Iohannis Calderini et domini Gasparis eius filii redacta*, con. 11 [De usuris Rubrica].
5. In c. Consuluit [*Dec. Greg.*, 5.19.10], quaest. 1, partis 3.
6. Argumentum: c. Statutum, s. proferendo, de rescriptis lib. 6 [*Liber Sextus*, 1.3.2] et notata per Baldum, Panormitarum et Felinum in c. 1, de testibus.
7. Lex Sed etsi, s. Consuluit, ff. de petitione haereditatis [Dig. 5.3.25.2] et c. cum in officiis, de testamentis [*Dec. Greg.*, 3.26.7].
8. Non enim ea quae praeter intentionem accidunt, sed natura rei est, in his inspiciendo, argumentum: lex Si quis nec causam, ff. de rebus creditis [Dig. 12.1.4], cum late ibi a Iasone traditis.
9. Lex ea, C. de alluvionibus [Cod. 7.41.3]; Panormitanus in cap. Propter, sub finem de locato [*Dec. Greg.*, 3.18.3].
10. Medina, *Codex de Restitutione et Contractibus*, tit. De causis in quas solent campsores lucrum augere, fol. 150 [fol. 158].
11. Soto, *De iustitia et iure*, lib. 7, quaest. 6, art. 2. [Cf. lib. 6, quaest. 13, art. 2, fol. 607 ff.].
12. *Consilia*, con. 11, De usuris [Rubrica].
13. C. De occidendis, 23, quaest. 5 [*Dec. Grat.*, 2.23.5.8]; c. Sacerdos 50 dist. [*Dec. Grat.*, 1.50.50].
14. Cajetan, *De cambiis*, cap. 7.
15. See section 31.

14

International Credit and Exchange

Summary

68. The last thing we say is that there is doubt among the learned men whether the dealings that are now carried out from Medina to Lisbon, Flanders, León, and other similar cities, and from these to Seville, Medina, and other such cities, which many survive on (whom I know) without any another activity, are licit. These dealings work in the following way (as I have learned at my expense): One who has money gives it at the end of the May fair in Medina del Campo (which ends at the end of July) for Lisbon, to be paid within a month, sometimes for an equal sum—that is, so many *ducats* for an equal sum, sometimes at 1 percent. Then in Lisbon, he gives it again for the fair of Medina in the month of October for 5 percent, 7 percent, or more for the October fair. At the end of this fair (which is at the end of December), he gives it again for Lisbon and the twentieth of January, sometimes for an equal sum, sometimes at 1 percent or more. Then, at the end of January, he gives it again for the fair of Villalón or of Medina de Rio Seco at 5 or 7 percent. Almost the same thing is done in other fairs of other cities and kingdoms for the kingdoms from here or others. Others give (according to Doctor Soto)[1] their money in Medina for Flanders, handing over 410 *maravedis* per *ducat* here to receive over there 360 per *ducat*, and there they give them again for Medina, giving there a *ducat* worth 300 *maravedis*, to receive here one of 375.

69. Against this deal:

First, it seems impossible to defend by way of buying or selling money because all purchase of something of a higher price for a lower one is illicit, according to Saint Thomas[2] and Scotus,[3] which, as we said above,[4] is well-known by everyone. In this deal, 100 *ducats* from Medina are bought in Lisbon for less than 95 and in Flanders for less than 90.

Second, it seems that inevitably it must be confessed that the purchase you do in Medina for Flanders or Lisbon, or in Lisbon and Flanders for Medina is a purchase of things of a greater price for a lower one. If it is a just price that you pay me 100 *ducats* in Medina for 100 or 101 that I should give you in Lisbon in one month, it shall be an unjust price if I give you 107 for the fair of October for only 100 that you give me in Lisbon. It seems that the 101 that I gave in Lisbon were not worth but 100 of yours in Medina, so your 100 from Lisbon cannot now be worth 107 of mine in Medina. If you have justly sold to me in past years in Lisbon 400 *maravedis* from Rome for 475, you have unjustly bought 400 *maravedis* from Lisbon for 400 that you give me in Rome. If for 410 that I give you in Medina, you justly sell me 360 that you have in Flanders, unjustly you sell me in Flanders 300 that you have there for 375 that I will give you here.

70. Third, what Doctor Soto[5] wants to admit for it cannot be admitted: by way of pure exchange and barter, considering that a lower sum of money in the land where there is great lack of it is worth more than another larger sum from a land where there is greater abundance. I say, then, that it cannot be admitted by this way. Doctor Soto expressly affirms that one cannot exchange licitly except what something is worth in one land for what something with the same value is worth in another land, and no more. The money that is given in Spain has to be worth as much and no more at the time when it is given as the money that for it will be given in Flanders is worth at that same time—whether it is given in eight days, or in a month, or in four, or in a year. Also, Soto himself says that there is no argument to explain the fact that you may licitly take in Spain, by sole way of exchange and barter, 410 *maravedis* for 360 that you will give me in Flanders, and then over there you give me 300 for 375 that I will give you here, because the exchange or barter from here to there, or from there to here, is unequal.

71. The fourth argument against this kind of deal—a well-studied conclusion of Saint Thomas,[6] Scotus,[7] and all of them—is that any deal is usury in which more is taken for reason of a longer period of waiting and delay. In the deal we are discussing it seems that more is taken for reasons of time and delay. The person who gives his *ducats* in Medina for Lisbon for a period of one month, gives them on equal terms, or at 1 percent. If he gives them for two months, he takes more; and for three, more. If he gives them in Lisbon for Medina when there are four months left for the fair, he takes more than if there were only three; if there were three, more than if there were not more than two; and if there were two, more than if there were no more than one. The person who gives money in Spain so that he gets paid back in Rome, gets the money cheaper if it is meant to be given back in three months than if it is to be given back later. For these reasons, we once thought that this deal was not possible.

72. In spite of all of these, we believe it is licit:

First, because, as Calderini says,[8] it seems absurd to condemn so many good merchants who carry this out, and to hurt everyone by condemning them.

Second, without this kind of deal, the deals with foreign kingdoms would disappear, and one's own kingdom would impoverish itself.

Third, the whole basis for this deal is that money that is absent is not worth as much as money that is present, as proved above,[9] and it is not worth as much when there is abundance and a great quantity of it than when there is lack and need of it, as was also proved above.[10] It is possible for the person who has money in Medina to buy or try getting by way of barter and exchange other money that is in Flanders for less than what it is worth over there, and then obtain it there, and buy or try to get by barter and other innominate contracts with people there other money that is in Medina for less than what it is worth there and in this way increase his assets. Also, someone who has money or credit in Flanders may buy money, or try to acquire it by barter, in Medina outside of the fair or at the beginning of the fair (if there is an abundance of it) for a cheaper price. Then he may buy or exchange it for a higher price at the fair, or at the end of it (if there is a greater lack) as long as he gives the just price for the absent money in present money and for the present money in absent money.

73. Fourth, from the previous reason we may resolve the first two arguments of the opponents, since from our previous argument it follows that admitting that there is no just purchase when there is no equality between the price and the merchandise, we should and must deny that, all else being equal, 100 that are present are not worth more than 100 that are absent. And we must deny that 100 that are absent cannot be bought for less than 100 that are present when the money from one place is worth the same as the money in the other place.

We must deny, too, the reason on which the opponents' arguments are based: that the just price for 100 *ducats* from Seville that are absent in Medina is 99 that are present, also 100 *ducats* that are present in Seville shall be in Seville the just price of 99 that are absent from Medina because rather 99 that are present in Seville shall be in Seville the just price for 100 that are absent from Medina.

We said, all else being equal, that one amount in its place of origin is worth as much as the other in its place of origin as is worth the money from Seville in Seville and the money from Medina in Medina. If one amount is worth more where it is than the others where they are, it may happen what happens every day: the absent amount is worth more than the present one, as commonly in our days the absent ones from Flanders have been worth more in Medina than the present ones from Medina in this city, and many times the absent ones from Lisbon have been worth more in Medina than the present ones from Medina in this city. This is the reason why we deny that if the price of 100 *ducats* that are absent from Lisbon are in Medina 100 present ones, then 100 present ones in Lisbon shall be there the just price of 100 absent ones from Medina. This is because the *ducats* from Lisbon are worth more in Lisbon than the *ducats* from Medina in Medina, as we said above.[11] That is why the *ducat* from Lisbon that is present is worth more in Lisbon than the absent *ducat* from Medina, for two reasons: for being present, and for being worth more over there by its very essence. So it is possible that the 100 that are present in Lisbon are worth much more than the 100 that are absent in Medina, although the very absence of the ones from Lisbon does not make them worth less in Medina than those of Medina for the compensation of the greatest value that the *ducats* have in Lisbon, as we have stated above.[12]

74. Fifth, this kind of deal is justified because our third reason also resolves the third argument of the opponents. From our third reason it follows that this deal may be admitted also by way of barter and by way of another innominate contract, as in I give so that you give me, because from this it follows that less money present is a just barter, exchange, and equivalent to more money that is present, deducing everything much as the issue about buying has been worked out. We declare, however, that Doctor Soto's manner of arguing cannot justify the deal that involves sending from one part to another, and from the other to another, as every day people deal, because of what we argued in the fourth argument against his manner of justification. The argument assumes three things that imply its total destruction:

1. the barter or exchange of money may not be carried out justly but between the money that already truly belongs to the two people who will carry out the exchange,
2. the absent money is not worth less than the present one, and
3. from these two it follows that the present money may not be bartered or exchanged for the absent money unless giving an amount for the present one that is worth where it is as much as the absent one is worth where it is.

From these three things a fourth one necessarily follows. If 100 *ducats* are a just barter and exchange in Medina for 90 from Flanders, no more, no less, then, too, 90 from Flanders, no more, no less, shall be a just price for 100 from Medina. From this follows a fifth conclusion, that is, that for this kind of deal nobody may increase his money or even keep it, except with great danger, expense, and care, which nobody cares about without some kind of profit. Consequently this deal would die off. Those who until now have practiced it would be forced to restitute what they have gained by carrying it out. Because we concluded earlier[13] that none of these three things may be proved by the law—rather, the opposite of them is in accordance with the law—we say that this deal, no more, no less, may be admitted by way of exchange, barter, or other innominate contract, just as we said earlier that it could be admitted by way of buying and selling.

75. Sixth, another argument that justifies this deal is that the opponents' fourth argument may be refuted by denying that in this deal (when it is carried out as it should be) something is taken for waiting or for a delay. Between just merchants, the time that there is between payment and payment is considered as if it were one day, as present time, to send the documents, get the payments ready, and carry them out, as Doctor Soto declared favorably,[14] although he did not give the reason for this, which seems to be the following. By law, some time must be given to carry out these things, and since it is not determined by law, it had to be determined by the good man's free will or law,[15] and custom has determined it, which becomes law where law is absent,[16] and has been induced by the will of prudent merchants so that it would be as we said, although sometimes less is enough and sometimes more is needed. The fourth argument of the opponents may also be refuted by considering that it is one thing to buy or sell something for its just price, or at least a pious one, that must be delivered three months from today, which is licit. It is licit to sell on credit,[17] and to sell what has to be born yet,[18] and even to barter,[19] as has been said above, which is what is done in this kind of deal. It is another thing to buy it for less than the just price (or at least pious) for reason of advancing the money, or selling it for more than the severe just price for giving it on credit, which are illicit, as the argument proves and as we declare.

Just as one can licitly buy or collect by barter before Christmas the yarn and herbs of the following year for their just price, so one may buy or collect by barter at the fair of Medina the money from Flanders for its just price so that it is paid in the first, second, or even third fair, as long as one does not take more than the rigorous just price for getting it back at a later date than what one would take for getting it in the first fairs. We concede, however, that every time that something significant is taken that is more than what is just, for the waiting and delay, the person sins and has the obligation to restitution.

76. We conclude, therefore, that this deal is licit, as long as these provisions are kept:

First, that the exchange not be feigned. That is, that the one who gives the money is willing and has the intention[20] of collecting it at the place from where it is taken, and he believes with reason that the one who takes it has or will have the money, extending a certificate or warrant to give it back there from where he takes it and promising that he will give it there.

Second, that for the absent money as much present money is given as is supposed to be just, and the price is not lowered too much for its absence. All of this should be estimated by the good man's own free will.[21]

Third, that no more money is taken for reason of a longer period of time until the moment in which the delivery or payments must be handed over than if it were to be delivered immediately where the payment is due.

The fourth provision derives from the previous one: that he not sell, barter, or give for more money when selling, bartering, or giving it for the second or third fair, than he gave for the first. We said more because if he decided to give it for the second and even for the third fair for what he would justly take until the payments of the first, then he can rightly do it, and it shall be a deed of charity and friendship; he would not be able to take more because even if what is given by way of true exchange or true interest may be given more expensively for two fairs than for one, and more expensively for three than for two, as was said above,[22] this is not so with the exchange by buying, bartering, or other innominate contract, which we refer to here.

77. From this we understand:

First, there are reasons to be uncertain regarding a case that they asked us about in Lisbon, in which a Castilian, who wanted to give there a certain quantity of *ducats* to a Portuguese merchant so that they were paid back to him with a certain profit in the first fair of Medina del Campo (which was to be held three or four months later) saw great advantage in having the money brought back to him in Castile. On the one hand, it seemed it was not possible because there did not seem to be any reason he would be able to take the profit.[23] Rather, it seemed that he had to give it to the merchant, as it suited the Castilian to bring his money from there to Medina, and the merchant was putting the skill and work of giving it to him in Medina, according to what we said about the justice of exchange by bills of exchange. On the other hand, there seems to be inequality and injustice in the merchant's giving as much here as he takes over there and, on top of that, giving of his skill and work and giving a profit[24] to the Castilian. The merchant did not want to give a profit if he had to give the money back soon after in Medina, but rather only if he had to give it from that time to three or four months, enjoying it in that time in between, and consequently was paying the profit for the delay in time, which is usury for what was said above[25] and elsewhere,[26] and Cajetan[27] seems to agree with this part.

78. Some however will be convinced by Doctor Soto to hold the opposite view, saying that if the merchant found it convenient to bring his money from Medina to Lisbon, as the other found it convenient to bring his to Medina, he could well take the profit that is taken for the exchange of bills of exchange. In this case Cajetan[28] also holds this, even if he does not argue it. We, however, believe there are five different ways by which the said Castilian may give the said *ducats*, four of which are without consideration of a longer or shorter period of time until the next fair, at least as a principal issue, and one of which includes this consideration.

The first, without said consideration, is by way of loan. The second, by exchange of bills of exchange with which the merchant may transfer his *ducats* here. The third, by way of his passing his *ducats* from Medina to the merchant there. The fourth, by way of buying, bartering, or any other innominate commutation of the merchant's absent *ducats* in Medina for his present ones in Lisbon. The fifth is with principal consideration of the time and deadline until the fair, by any of the said ways, taking from him more or less according to the greater or lesser time that there was until them.

In the first case—wanting to give them by way of loan and with a pact or principal intention of having them paid in Medina—he was a usurer because, by loaning, he wanted to gain a benefit, that is, the obligation of making him pay in Medina with a profit, having lent them in Lisbon—which is a benefit estimated in money.[29] If, instead, he wanted to lend them to him without such pact and intention of making him pay unavoidably in Medina, but there in Lisbon, so much for so much, or in Medina with that profit as a reward for what the money was worth in excess there than in Medina, he could then licitly take that extra amount if the *ducats* were worth so much more there than here, for what we said above.[30]

In the second case, if he wanted to give them by way of exchange of bills of exchange so that the merchant transferred his money to Medina, the Castilian was forced to give the other a reward for this, for what we said earlier. This is true even if it were possible in the contract to agree that for his salary he could take the excess of what the money was worth there in relation to here, or a part of it, whatever was just, for what we said above.[31]

In the third case, if he wanted to give them by way of transferring the money from here to there, the merchant could take the salary corresponding to what the banker would take justly for transferring them for him.

In the fourth case, if he wanted to give them by way of buying, bartering, or other innominate contract of "I give so you give me," he would be able to take more for two reasons: because the merchant's money was absent and thus was worth less, and because the money was worth more there than the money here, as we have said above.[32]

In the fifth case, if he wanted to give the *ducats* by any one of the ways described above, with principal consideration of the time that remained until the payment, wanting to take more or less according to the longer or shorter period of time, we say undoubtedly that this was illicit for him. We have concluded above[33] that not only the contract for lending but all other contracts in which more or less is taken for a longer or shorter period until the payment, are formal or virtual usury.

79. The second thing[34] that follows is that proportionately a distinction has to be made when someone else wants to give money in Medina, where it is worth less, for Lisbon, or for Flanders, where it is worth more; or in Seville for Medina, where it is worth the same, which to avoid extending ourselves, we shall not explain.

The third thing follows and is what should be said about Saint Antonino's[35] principle: the usurer is the exchanger or banker who gives someone in Rome 100 or 1,000 *ducats* for his commercial dealings, to be paid from today in six months in Paris with a pact that he pay him there 5 or 8 percent more. This is understood, too, by Silvestre,[36] and both are approved by the most learned "Licentiate" Gregorio Lopez,[37] who is satisfied with that title, in spite of belonging to the Council of the Indies, and deserving, too, of the title "Doctor," as is manifest in the great work and erudition with which he has composed the very apt, discreet, and beneficial glosses on all the Seven Certifications[38] that he published and printed last year with great benefit to the republic while he was in this same cell as we are, although not as invisible as we are.

And this is what should be said about Antonino's principle:

First, that it is true because in that contract, according to what it stipulates, 5 or 8 percent is taken for the delay and consideration of the time that there is between the loan and the payment, which is obvious usury.

Second, that such a contract could not be carried out licitly by way of loan to Paris—even if the time and delay were not taken into account—but could be carried out to Spain because, as nothing is to be desired for a loan and money is worth more in France than in Rome, it is illicit for two reasons: More is taken due to the place where the money is to be paid, and an extra 5 or 8 percent are taken. For Spain, it would be possible by not taking those extra 5 or 8 percent, inasmuch as money from here is worth less than money from there to be paid promptly here.

Third, that such a contract may be carried out licitly by way of buying, bartering, or another innominate contract by giving there, considering the time factor, those 100 present *ducats* for another similar amount and some more absent ones, as long as the said[39] four conditions are kept. He would be able to take more if he gave them for Spain than if he gave them for France because Spain is farther away from Rome than France and, for this reason, the absent ones from Spain are worth less in Rome than the absent ones from France, for what was said above,[40] and also because money is worth less in Spain than in Rome and in France more than in Rome and Spain. This was, according to our way of thinking, what Silvestre[41] meant when he said that this contract, as it was carried out, was usurious but that it was possible to carry it out properly.

80. Now follows the final issue: It is not exchange but usury under the name of exchange when those who, once the fair has started and the time of payment has arrived, give the debtors (who do not pay) a delay and more time until the next fair, as long as they pay an amount for the new exchange, as Cajetan[42] notes well. It cannot be denied that by way of exchanging for an interest the exchangers could take from the debtors the amount that for reason of them not paying when they should, the exchangers stop from gaining with true exchanges that they would carry out if they had that money, as was said above.[43]

This is what, with due correction, with all honesty and without evil deception before God, we have considered about exchanges. This is the limit to where those involved in such exchanges can extend their profit. We have extended it as much as possible in order to justly defend the souls, honor, and fortune of so many important and honorable people. We hope that those who are not included in this deal do not feel any envy toward those who make a living from it, even if they are noble. We advise the confessors of those who live from these kind of deals to solemnly advise them against feigned exchanges and interests, and to persuade them that the temptations that arise from these deals make their walk toward Paradise one that passes over high and rocky grades, and that the tumbles that come from the great love and attraction of great profits may easily hurl them down deep ravines of sins that they cannot get out of and into such thick bramble patches of restitutions from which they cannot rid themselves.

May the One who was crowned with a crown of brambles and thorns raise and rid those who have already fallen into them, and also those of us who have just as many times fallen into others, and raise us all to the most boundless heights of the heavens for love of his very glorious Mother Queen of them all, the eighth day of whose most joyful visitation the Catholic Church today celebrates. Amen.

Salamanca, 8th of July, in the 1556th year
of the One born of the Virgin Mother

Notes

1. Soto, *De iustitia et iure*, lib. 7, quaest. 5, art. 2. Cf. lib. 6, quaest. 12, art. 2 [fol. 594].
2. Thomas, *Summa theologicae*, II-II, quaest. 77, art. 1, receptum ab omnibus.
3. Scotus, *Quaestiones in quattuor libros sententiarum*, lib. 4, dist. 15, quaest. 2.
4. See sections 14, 24, and 41.
5. Soto, *De iustitia et iure*, lib. 7, quaest, 5. art. 2. Cf. lib. 6, quaest. 12, art. 2 [fol. 599].
6. Thomas, *Summa theologicae*, II-II, quaest. 78, art. 2, ad. 7.
7. Scotus, *Quaestiones*, lib. 4, dist. 15, quaest. 2, art. 2 dictumque fuit supra eodem, no. 14 et 24, et in Azpilcueta, *Comentario Resolutorio de Usuras*, cap. 1, 14, quaest. 3 [*Dec. Grat.*, 2.16.3.1], no. 26, et probatur in c. Ad nostram, de emptione [*Dec. Greg.*, 5.17.3], et in c. In civitate, supra eodem [*Dec. Greg.*, 3.17.5].
8. Giovanni Calderini and Gaspar Calderini, *Consilia domini Iohannis Calderini et domini Gasparis eius filii redacta*, con. 11 [De usuris Rubrica].
9. See section 62 and following.
10. See section 51.
11. See section 60 and following.
12. See section 63.
13. See sections 14 and 62.
14. Soto, *De iustitia et iure*, lib. 7, quaest. 5, art. 2. Cf. lib. 6, quaest. 12, art. 2 [fol. 594].
15. Argumentum, lex 1, ff. de iure deliberandi [Dig. 28.8.1], et c. De causis, de officio [et potestate iudicis] delegati [*Dec. Greg.*, 1.29.4].
16. C. Consuetudo, 1, dist. 1 [*Dec. Grat.*, 1.1.5], lex De quibus, ff. de legibus [Dig. 1.3.32].

17. S. venditae, Institutionum, De rerum divisione [*Inst.* 2.1.1.41].

18. Lex Nec emptio, ff. de contrahenda emptione, cum glossa [Dig. 18.1.8].

19. See section 14.

20. Alioquin enim non esset emptio nec permutatio, argumentum: lex Non omnis, ff. de rebus creditis [Dig. 3.12.19], C. cum super, de officio [et potestate indicis] delegati [*Dec. Greg.*, 1.19.23].

21. Argumentum: Lex 1, ff. de iure deliberandi [Dig. 28.8.1], c. De causis, de officio [et potestate indicis] delegati [*Dec. Greg.*, 1.29.4].

22. See section 34.

23. Usurpatio autem sine titulo iusto illicita est, c. Poenale, 14, quaest. 5 [*Dec. Grat.*, 2.14.5.13].

24. At omnis contractus, in quo no servatur aequalitas, est illicitus, ut ait Scotus, *Quaestiones*, lib. 4, dist. 15, quaest. 2, art. 2 [fol. 94], et Paulo ante no. 23 et 24 est dictum.

25. See section 23.

26. Azpilcueta, *Comentario Resolutorio de Usuras*, cap. 1, 14, quaest. 3, no. 26.

27. Cajetan, *De cambiis*, cap. Finales [cap. 8].

28. Cajetan, *De cambiis*, cap. 8.

29. Ac per consequutionem, *usura*, c. 1, 2 et 3, 14, quaest. 3 [*Dec. Grat.*, 2.14.1–3], ut latius diximus in commentario dicto c. 1, n. 5.

30 See section 61.

31. See section 21.

32. See section 61.

33. See section 47.

34. Ed. note: The first point in this argument appears in section 77.

35. Antonino, *Summa theologicae*, 2 parte, tit. 1, c. 7, s. 50.

36. Silvestre, *Sylvestrina suma, qua summa summarum merito nuncupatur*, verb. *usura* 4, quaest. 13.

37. Lopez, *Las Siete Partidas*, lex 31, quinta Partita, tit. 11.

38. Ed. note: Cf. chapter 2, note 10.

39. See section 64.

40. See section 64.

41. Silvestre, *Suma*, verb. *usura* 4, quaest. 13.

42. Cajetan, *De cambiis*, cap. 7.

43. See section 34.

About the Contributors

Jordan J. Ballor (Dr. theol., University of Zurich) is a research fellow at the Acton Institute for the Study of Religion & Liberty and serves as executive editor of the *Journal of Markets & Morality*. He is also the author of *Covenant, Causality, and Law: A Study in the Theology of Wolfgang Musculus* (Vandenhoeck & Ruprecht, 2012) and *Ecumenical Babel: Confusing Economic Ideology and the Church's Social Witness* (Christian's Library Press, 2010).

Jeannine Emery has a degree in Spanish literature and a master's in nonfiction writing. She works as an editor and translator in both English and Spanish. She lives in Buenos Aires, Argentina.

Stephen J. Grabill (PhD, Calvin Theological Seminary) serves as senior research scholar in theology and director of programs at the Acton Institute for the Study of Religion & Liberty. He is editor emeritus of the *Journal of Markets & Morality*, as well as author of *Rediscovering the Natural Law in Reformed Theological Ethics* (Eerdmans, 2006) and editor of *Sourcebook in Late-Scholastic Monetary Theory* (Lexington, 2007).

Rodrigo Muñoz is professor in the faculty of theology at the University of Navarra, Spain, in the areas of moral theology and Catholic social teaching. His research interests include the economic teachings of the theologians of the sixteenth-century "School of Salamanca," the connection between justice and charity in modern society, and more recently, questions concerning Christianity and politics and religion in the public square. He is the author of *Moral y economía en la obra de Martín de Azpilcueta* (EUNSA, 1998) and a contributing editor of *Religión, sociedad moderna y razón práctica* (EUNSA, 2012).

Christian's LIBRARY PRESS

Founded in 1979 by Gerard Berghoef and Lester DeKoster, **CHRISTIAN'S LIBRARY PRESS** has been committed to publishing influential texts on church leadership, the vocation of work, and stewardship for more than thirty years. During that time Berghoef and DeKoster wrote significant works including *The Deacons Handbook*, *The Elders Handbook*, and *God's Yardstick*, which still are in demand today. After the passing of Lester DeKoster in 2009, the imprint is now administered by the Acton Institute for the Study of Religion & Liberty. For more information about Christian's Library Press, visit www.clpress.com.

ACTON INSTITUTE

With its commitment to pursue a society that is free and virtuous, the **ACTON INSTITUTE FOR THE STUDY OF RELIGION & LIBERTY** is a leading voice in the international environmental and social policy debate. With offices in Grand Rapids, Michigan, and Rome, Italy, as well as affiliates in four other nations around the world, the Acton Institute is uniquely positioned to comment on the sound economic and moral foundations necessary to sustain humane environmental and social policies. The Acton Institute is a nonprofit, ecumenical think tank working internationally to "promote a free and virtuous society characterized by individual liberty and sustained by religious principles." For more on the Acton Institute, please visit www.acton.org.

Sources in Early Modern Economics, Ethics, and Law

Jordan J. Ballor and Stephen J. Grabill, General Editors

Books in This Series

A Treatise on the Alteration of Money
Juan de Mariana
Translated by Patrick T. Brannan • Annotations by Stephen J. Grabill
Introduction by Alejandro A. Chafuen

On the Law in General
Girolamo Zanchi
Translated by Jeffrey J. Veenstra • Introduction by Stephen J. Grabill

On Law and Power
Johannes Althusius
Translated by Jeffrey J. Veenstra • Introductions by Stephen J. Grabill and John Witte Jr.

On Exchange and Usury
Thomas Cajetan
Translated by Patrick T. Brannan • Introduction by Raymond de Roover

On Righteousness, Oaths, and Usury
Wolfgang Musculus
Translated by Todd M. Rester • Introduction by Jordan J. Ballor

On Exchange
Martín de Azpilcueta
Translated by Jeannine Emery • Introduction by Rodrigo Muñoz

A Treatise on Money
Luis de Molina
Translated by Jeannine Emery • Introduction by Rudolf Schuessler

The Mosaic Polity
Franciscus Junius
Translated by Todd M. Rester • Edited by Andrew M. McGinnis

Of the Law of Nature
Matthew Hale
Edited by David S. Sytsma

On Sale, Securities, and Insurance
Leonardus Lessius
Translated by Wim Decock and Nicholas De Sutter • Introduction by Wim Decock

Made in the USA
Monee, IL
04 November 2026

67376413R00105